Focus on Phonics - 4

by Gail V. L

Other Vowel Sounds and Consonant Spellings

Student Workbook

Correlated to
Laubach Way to Reading
Skill Book 4

EACH ONE TEACH ONE

ISBN 0-88336-453-0

© Copyright 1985, 1991

New Readers Press
Publishing Division of Laubach Literacy International
Box 131, Syracuse, New York 13210

Designed by Kay Koschnick

Illustrated by Caris Lester and Chris Steenwerth

Printed in the United States of America

20 19 18 17 16 15 14 13 12 11

10 9 8 7 6

Practice 1-A: Long *u* = /ū/

1   **Short u**   **Long u**

u   **ū**

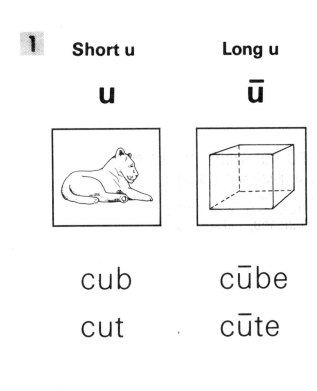

cub   cūbe

cut   cūte

2   Read the words.

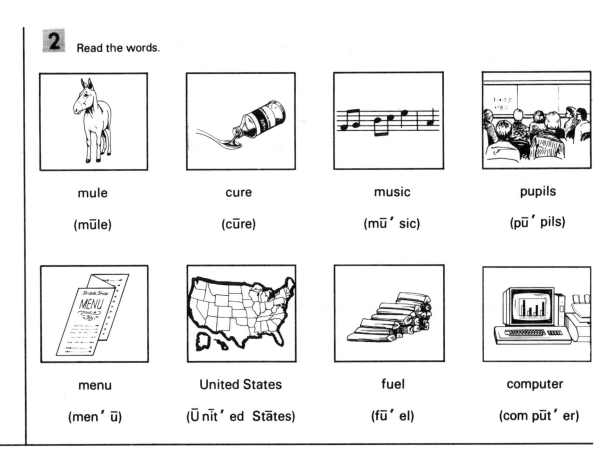

mule   cure   music   pupils

(mūle)   (cūre)   (mū′ sic)   (pū′ pils)

menu   United States   fuel   computer

(men′ ū)   (Ū nīt′ ed Stātes)   (fū′ el)   (com pūt′ er)

3   Read these sentences.   **Review words:** human, huge, use (ūz)

1. The music teacher has ten pupils.

2. We use gas for fuel in the United States.

3. These pills will cure the sick man.

4. Order your meal from this menu.

5. Put another ice cube in the drink.

6. The little puppy is cute.

7. The mule is carrying a huge pack on its back.

8. Computers do jobs faster than humans.

Practice 1-B: *u-e* = /ū/

1

use

cure

huge

-u_e

2 Read the words.

use	cure	cute
fuse	pure	
refuse	secure	huge
confuse		
excuse	fume	mule
accuse	perfume	
amuse	volume	cube
abuse		

3 Write the word you hear.

1. _____   10. _____
2. _____   11. _____
3. _____   12. _____
4. _____   13. _____
5. _____   14. _____
6. _____   15. _____
7. _____   16. _____
8. _____   17. _____
9. _____   18. _____

4 Read the sentences.   **Review words:** human, computer

1. Did Dr. Hill use this drug to cure her?

2. Computers take jobs away from humans.

3. Excuse me for stepping on your toe.

4. That cute little puppy amuses us.

5. Turn up the volume so I can hear.

6. "You abuse your son," I accused Jan.

   "He does not feel safe and secure."

7. I refuse to let her use my perfume.

8. Is this air pure? I smell gas fumes.

9. He changed the fuse when it burned out.

10. Put two ice cubes in each glass.

11. He refuses to ride on that old mule.

12. My money is secure in this huge safe.

13. These street signs confuse me.

14. Put that huge volume back on the shelf.

15. Did he accuse her of stealing?

5 **Two ways to say** use, excuse, abuse

Use = /ūz/ in action words.

Otherwise, use = /ūs/. Compare:

/z/ May I use your telephone?

/s/ Computers have many uses.

/z/ The boy abuses his pup.

/s/ Ann helps fight child abuse.

/z/ Please excuse me. I have to leave.

/s/ There is no excuse for being late.

3

Practice 2: *ue* and *ew* = /ū/

1

argue

-ue

few

-ew

2 Read the words.

ue = /ū/	ew = /ū/
argue	few
value	mew
rescue	pew
barbecue	view
continue	review
	interview
	nephew

3 Write the word you hear.

1. _____ 9. _____

2. _____ 10. _____

3. _____ 11. _____

4. _____ 12. _____

5. _____

6. _____

7. _____

8. _____

4 Read the sentences. **Review words:** Hugh, cousin, refuse, reunion, lovely, minute, aunt

1. Hugh will barbecue ribs on the grill.

2. My nephew loves rock music.

3. Did he rescue his aunt from the fire?

4. My cousin and I used to argue a lot.

5. What a lovely view of the lake!

6. Every year, your home goes up in value.

7. May I interview you for a few minutes?

8. A few people sat in the church pews.

9. The music will continue for a minute.

10. Hugh met a lovely girl at the barbecue.

11. Her cousin has a job interview.

12. My aunt heard the cat mew.

13. Review your notes for the test.

14. I saw my nephew at the family reunion.

15. A rescue boat came into view.

16. A few men continued to argue.

5 Circle the letter for the vowel sound you hear.

1. u ū   9. u ū

2. u ū   10. u ū

3. u ū   11. u ū

4. u ū   12. u ū

5. u ū   13. u ū

6. u ū   14. u ū

7. u ū   15. u ū

8. u ū   16. u ū

Practice 3-A: *oo = /oo/* as in *-ool, -oon, -ood*

1

pool
school
-ool

noon
soon
-oon

food
-ood

2 Write the letters and say the word.

c _____ ool   m _____ oon

f _____ ool   n _____ oon

p _____ ool   s _____ oon

t _____ ool   sp _____ oon

dr _____ ool

st _____ ool

sp _____ ool   f _____ ood

sch _____ ool   m _____ ood

3 Read the words.

tool	soon
spool	moon
fool	spoon
drool	noon
cool	
school	
pool	mood
stool	food

4 Write the word you hear.

1. _____   9. _____

2. _____   10. _____

3. _____   11. _____

4. _____   12. _____

5. _____   13. _____

6. _____   14. _____

7. _____

8. _____

5 Read the sentences.   **Review words:** O'Toole, afternoon, since, together, haven't

1. Our school has a big swimming pool.

2. Jane O'Toole is in a bad mood.

3. He was a fool to drop out of school.

4. It will be cool this afternoon.

5. Our baby eats his food with a spoon.

   Then he drools on his bib.

6. Please bring my tools back soon.

7. School teachers eat together at noon.

8. Mrs. O'Toole buys two spools of thread.

9. I haven't seen her since noon.

10. Hugh sat on the little stool.

11. We play pool together every afternoon.

12. At night, you can see the moon.

13. My aunt will serve the food soon.

14. He tried to fool me, but I stayed cool.

15. We haven't got the tools for this job.

6 Circle the letter or letters for the vowel sound you hear.

1. u   oo   9. u   oo

2. u   oo   10. u   oo

3. u   oo   11. u   oo

4. u   oo   12. u   oo

5. u   oo   13. u   oo

6. u   oo   14. u   oo

7. u   oo   15. u   oo

8. u   oo   16. u   oo

Practice 3-B: *oo* = /oo/ as in *-oop, -oot, -ook*

1

stoop

-oop

boot

shoot

-oot

spook

-ook

2 Write the letters and say the word.

c ____ oop		b ____ oot	
h ____ oop		h ____ oot	
l ____ oop		l ____ oot	
dr ____ oop		r ____ oot	
tr ____ oop		t ____ oot	
sn ____ oop		sh ____ oot	
sc ____ oop		sc ____ oot	
st ____ oop			
sw ____ oop		sp ____ ook	

3 Read the words.

snoop	root
hoop	shoot
swoop	boot
troop	toot
coop	scoot
droop	hoot
scoop	loot
loop	
stoop	spook

4 Write the word you hear.

1. _____	10. _____
2. _____	11. _____
3. _____	12. _____
4. _____	13. _____
5. _____	14. _____
6. _____	15. _____
7. _____	16. _____
8. _____	17. _____
9. _____	

5 Read the sentences.   **New word:** chicken   **Review words:** afraid, those, through

1. Those plants have short, thick roots.

2. Water those roses. They are drooping.

3. The robber got away with the loot.

4. Put the belt through the loops.

5. My pup can jump through a hoop.

6. Feed the chickens in the chicken coop.

7. She stoops to wipe off her boots.

8. The army troops were shooting.

9. I told the pup, "Scoot!" He ran off.

10. The pupils trooped through the school.

11. We heard a bird hoot in the night.

12. He is afraid of ghosts and spooks.

13. The driver toots the car horn.

14. Hugh was snooping through my desk.

15. A big bird swooped down on the chicken.

16. Give me two scoops of ice cream.

6 Circle the letter or letters for the vowel sound you hear.

1. u oo		9. u oo	
2. u oo		10. u oo	
3. u oo		11. u oo	
4. u oo		12. u oo	
5. u oo		13. u oo	
6. u oo		14. u oo	
7. u oo		15. u oo	
8. u oo		16. u oo	

Practice 3-C: *oo* = /oo/ as in *-oom, -oo, -oof*

1

room

-oom

too

-oo

roof

-oof

2 Write the letters and say the word.

b ___ oom	b ___ oo
l ___ oom	c ___ oo
r ___ oom	m ___ oo
z ___ oom	t ___ oo
bl ___ oom	z ___ oo
gl ___ oom	sh ___ oo
br ___ oom	
gr ___ oom	r ___ oof
	pr ___ oof

3 Read the words.

room	zoo
bloom	moo
zoom	boo
boom	shoo
groom	too
loom	coo
broom	
gloom	proof
	roof

4 Write the word you hear.

1. _____	10. _____
2. _____	11. _____
3. _____	12. _____
4. _____	13. _____
5. _____	14. _____
6. _____	15. _____
7. _____	16. _____
8. _____	
9. _____	

5 Read the sentences. **Review words:** roommate, bedroom, listen

1. Roses bloom in the spring.

2. We want to go to the zoo, too.

3. The gun went off with a boom.

4. I have proof that he stole the money.

5. Sweep up the dirt with this broom.

6. She uses a loom to weave the yarn.

7. My roommate jumps when I yell "Boo!"

8. Our six-bedroom home has lots of room.

9. Listen to the baby coo.

10. The groom gave a ring to his bride.

11. We listened to the rain on the roof.

12. The car zoomed up the street.

13. I was filled with gloom when he died.

14. I'm too tired to clean my room.

15. The farmer heard a moo from the barn.

16. She tried to shoo the flies away.

6 **Homonyms:** too and two

The dog is hungry and thirsty, too.

He works at too many jobs.

We will be gone for two weeks.

They have _____ children.

I ate my cake and hers, _____.

He was _____ angry to speak.

Hugh paid me _____ dollars.

Practice 3-D: *oo* = /oo/ as in *-ooth, -oose, -ooze, -oove, -oost*

1

tooth
-ooth

loose
-oose

snooze
-ooze

groove
-oove

boost
-oost

2 Write the letters and say the word.

b	___ ooth	ch	___ oose
t	___ ooth		
			ooze
sm	___ ooth	b	___ ooze
		sn	___ ooze
g	___ oose		
l	___ oose	gr	___ oove
m	___ oose		
n	___ oose	b	___ oost

3 Read the words.

tooth	choose
booth	
	booze
smooth	ooze
	snooze
moose	
goose	groove
noose	
loose	boost

4 Write the word you hear.

1. _____   10. _____

2. _____   11. _____

3. _____   12. _____

4. _____   13. _____

5. _____

6. _____

7. _____

8. _____

9. _____

5 Read the sentences.   **Review words:** Hoover, Sunday, aren't

1. I don't know which one to choose.

2. These roads aren't very smooth.

3. Jimmy Hoover has a loose tooth.

4. Did the hunter shoot the goose?

5. I take a snooze on Sunday afternoons.

6. She stepped into a phone booth.

7. Hugh drinks too much booze.

8. We aren't going moose hunting.

9. The mud oozes between my toes.

10. Give me a boost over the fence.

11. The plane made a smooth landing.

12. Use this rope to make a noose.

13. We choose to let our pup run loose.

14. Dr. Hoover will fill my tooth.

15. We'll have a goose for Sunday dinner.

16. The shelf fits into these grooves.

6 **Homonyms:** too and to

He took pens and pencils, too.

It's too late to call her.

The shop is open from 8 to 5.

Take that box to the office.

We need a doctor _____ help us.

That skirt is _____ big for her.

Hugh worked from three _____ five.

She went _____ the zoo, _____.

8

Practice 4-A: *u-e* = /oo/

1

June
rule
flute

-u_e

2 Read the words.

June	nude	Bruce
tune	rude	truce
prune	crude	spruce
	include	reduce
		produce
flute	tube	introduce
brute		
salute	rule	assume
pollute		costume

3 Write the word you hear.

1. _____ 10. _____ 19. _____

2. _____ 11. _____ 20. _____

3. _____ 12. _____ 21. _____

4. _____ 13. _____

5. _____ 14. _____

6. _____ 15. _____

7. _____ 16. _____

8. _____ 17. _____

9. _____ 18. _____

4 Read the sentences.   **New words:** Luke, Duke, dog   **Review words:** flag, upset

1. The rude men refuse to salute the flag.

2. Did Bruce introduce you to Duke?

3. He upsets people with his crude jokes.

4. I can fit into the costume if I reduce.

5. June buys a tube of hand cream.

6. City rules say dogs must not run free.

7. Bruce is eating nuts and prunes.

8. Luke plays a tune on his flute.

9. June's dog Duke is a big brute.

10. In June, the armies agreed to a truce.

11. Dog food is on sale at a reduced price.

12. Luke assumes that I know the rules.

13. It was rude not to include her.

14. Spruce trees are used to produce paper.

15. Smoke and gas fumes pollute our air.

16. Luke was swimming in the nude.

5 Homonyms: Fill in the blanks with to, two, or too.

1. Did he speak _____ his wife?

2. This picture is _____ dark.

3. Luke left for _____ weeks.

4. We sent letters _____ our friends.

5. It's _____ soon _____ quit.

6. He came here _____ help me.

7. The pen sells for _____ dollars.

8. She drives a car and a truck, _____ .

9

Practice 4-B: *ue* = /oo/

1

blue

true

-ue

2 Read the words.

sue	issue
Sue	tissue
due	
blue	avenue
clue	
glue	dues
true	Tuesday

3 Write the word you hear.

1. _____   10. _____
2. _____   11. _____
3. _____   12. _____
4. _____
5. _____
6. _____
7. _____
8. _____
9. _____

4 Read the sentences.   **Review words:** July, Thursday, month, union, goes, U.S.

1. Sue has on a lovely blue dress.

2. July is the month after June.

3. That is a lie! It's not true.

4. The U.S. flag is red, white, and blue.

5. The police are looking for clues.

6. Have you read last month's issue?

7. Squeeze some glue out of the tube.

8. The bill is due to be paid on Tuesday.

9. My van hit a blue car on First Avenue.

   The driver yelled, "I'll sue you!"

10. He uses a tissue to wipe his nose.

11. Sue goes to school on Tuesday nights.

12. We pay union dues on Thursday, July 1.

13. He traces the picture on tissue paper.

14. We have many issues to vote on.

15. Sue is a true friend when I feel blue.

5 **Homonyms:** Fill in the blanks with to, two, or too.

1. Sue's dog barks _____ much.

2. The shop is _____ miles from here.

3. Take that cash _____ the bank.

4. We met from three _____ five.

5. _____ of us went _____ the city.

6. I am out of a job, _____ .

7. Turn _____ the right.

8. This school is _____ big for me.

10

Practice 5: *ew* = /oo/

1

new
chew
grew
-ew

2 Write the letters and say the word.

d	___ ew	dr	___ ew
n	___ ew	gr	___ ew
kn	___ ew	st	___ ew
J	___ ew	thr	___ ew
ch	___ ew	scr	___ ew
bl	___ ew		
fl	___ ew		
br	___ ew		
cr	___ ew		

3 Read the words.

blew	threw
stew	chew
knew	drew
crew	screw
dew	new
grew	
Jew	newspaper
flew	jewel
brew	sewer

4 Write the word you hear.

1. _____	10. _____
2. _____	11. _____
3. _____	12. _____
4. _____	13. _____
5. _____	14. _____
6. _____	15. _____
7. _____	16. _____
8. _____	17. _____
9. _____	

5 Read the sentences.   Review words: news, Lewis, Luke, until

1. The wind blew his new hat off.

2. I knew that Luke stole the jewels.

3. Stir the stew until it gets hot.

4. I haven't got any chewing gum.

5. The birds flew high in the sky.

6. The work crew cleaned the sewers.

7. Mrs. Lewis will brew some tea.

8. Have you seen the picture he drew?

9. Luke knew the friends I grew up with.

10. Turn the screw until it is tight.

11. She has a new baby! That's good news!

12. Lewis threw the newspaper on the porch.

13. The plane flew with a large crew.

14. Many Jews do not eat pork.

15. The dew makes the grass wet.

16. An angry mob grew. People threw rocks.

6 Homonyms: new and knew

We bought a new car.

The school board hired a new teacher.

I knew your uncle years ago.

June knew the answers.

She started a _____ job.

He _____ our phone number.

I _____ the people at the party.

Luke got a stain on his _____ shirt.

11

Practice 6-A: *u* = /oo/ **in Longer Words**

1

tutor

stupid

ruin

u

2 Read the words.

tuna	(tu′ na)	truly	(tru′ ly)
tuba	(tu′ ba)	ruby	(ru′ by)
tutor	(tu′ tor)	brutal	(bru′ tal)
tulip	(tu′ lip)	cruel	(cru′ el)
tumor	(tu′ mor)	ruin	(ru′ in)
student	(stu′ dent)	rumor	(ru′ mor)
stupid	(stu′ pid)		
duty	(du′ ty)		
duel	(du′ el)		

3 Write the word you hear.

1. _____   10. _____

2. _____   11. _____

3. _____   12. _____

4. _____   13. _____

5. _____   14. _____

6. _____   15. _____

7. _____

8. _____

9. _____

4 Read the sentences.   **Review words:** Judy, Newman, avenue

1. Judy knew the student was not stupid.

   He just needed a tutor to help him.

2. That man is cruel and brutal.

3. Your ruby ring is truly lovely.

4. A cruel rumor may ruin his good name.

5. The tulips bloomed in the spring.

6. I'm a tutor at a school on Lake Avenue.

7. Judy Newman plays a tuba in the band.

8. I ate a tuna sandwich for lunch.

9. It's my duty to stop that rumor.

10. Tell me what you truly think.

11. Mr. Newman has a brain tumor.

12. The weeds ruined my tulip garden.

13. That brutal man wants to fight a duel.

14. Students have a duty to follow rules.

15. One stupid mistake can ruin us!

5 **Homonyms:** <u>blew</u> and <u>blue</u>

The wind <u>blew</u> the curtains.

A bomb <u>blew</u> up.

The sky is a beautiful <u>blue</u>.

I'm feeling depressed and <u>blue</u>.

A storm _____ the roof off.

She wore a _____ coat and hat.

The plane crashed and then _____ up.

I felt _____ after I heard bad news.

Practice 6-B: Irregular /oo/: *o*

1 Read the words.

o

do	whom	move	movie
to		remove	
into	whose	prove	
two	lose	improve	
who		approve	

2 Write the word you hear.

1. _____   8. _____

2. _____   9. _____

3. _____   10. _____

4. _____   11. _____

5. _____   12. _____

6. _____   13. _____

7. _____   14. _____

3 Read the sentences.   **Review words:** birthday, Wednesday, begin, dirt

1. Who will win the game? Who will lose?

2. The movie on Wednesday begins at two.

3. What can we do to improve our work?

4. Please remove your hat.

5. Whose home did you move into?

6. I can prove that you stole it.

7. Whom do you like best?

8. Do they approve of what he does?

9. Move into the room over there.

10. Whose birthday is on Wednesday?

11. He can prove that what he says is true.

12. This soap will remove that dirt.

13. He goes to movies we don't approve of.

14. I hope your spelling begins to improve.

15. Her son will be two on his birthday.

16. Whose pen is this? Did you lose yours?

4 **Homonyms:** do and due

Do you ever go fishing?

I cannot do my homework.

The payment is due tomorrow.

They are due to arrive soon.

The train is _____ at noon.

_____ they like to swim?

She did not _____ her math.

Rent is _____ on the first of the month.

Practice 6-C: Irregular /oo/: *ou, oe, u, ui*

1
Read the words.

ou		oe	u	ui
you	through	shoe	Ruth	suit
youth	wound	canoe	truth	fruit
soup	route		flu	juice
group	Louis			cruise
				bruise

2
Write the word you hear.

1. _____
2. _____
3. _____
4. _____
5. _____
6. _____

7. _____
8. _____
9. _____
10. _____
11. _____
12. _____

13. _____
14. _____
15. _____
16. _____
17. _____
18. _____

3
Read the sentences.   **Review words:** Luther, Newman, January, can't

1. Did Ruth and Luther tell you the truth?

2. That route leads you through the city.

3. Louis wore a blue suit and black shoes.

4. Luther had bad wounds and bruises.

5. Mrs. Newman is through with her soup.

6. Our youth group went on a canoe trip.

7. Ruth has the flu. She can't eat much.

   She just has some soup and fruit juice.

8. We plan to go on a cruise in January.

9. Mr. Newman spilled juice on his suit.

10. A group of farmers picked the fruit.

11. I can't lie. I must speak the truth.

12. In January, Louis was sick with the flu.

13. One youth in the group was wounded.

14. I can't find any shoes to suit me.

15. The cruise ship follows this route.

4
Homonyms: route and root

This route leads into town.

That plant has long, thin roots.

Add an ending to the root word.

They cheer and root for the winners.

We will _____ for our team.

A tree gets water through its _____s.

This is the _____ to follow.

Find the _____ word.

Practice 7-A: Review of /ū/ and /oo/

1   Look at the picture and say the word. Then write the word.

_____   _____   _____

_____   _____   _____

2   Use these words to fill in the blanks:

truth   choose   confuse   argue

stew   blue   flute   mood

1. Luke spilled glue on his new _____ suit.

2. A few people in the group continued to _____.

3. Ruth was rude to me. She is in a bad _____.

4. Judy takes _____ lessons at the music school.

5. My nephew Bruce refused to tell me the _____.

6. The tutor tried not to _____ the students.

7. Which food did you _____ from the menu?

Did you order beef _____, chicken soup, or barbecued ribs?

3   Circle all the words that are the same as the first one.

boot	hoot	boot	loot	bout	boo	boot	tool
cute	cute	cue	cut	cute	cure	truce	acute
drew	brew	word	drew	grew	drew	dew	draw
rule	lure	rule	rude	cruel	mule	ruler	rule
lose	loose	loss	lose	sole	lose	louse	loser

4   Make at least 10 words with these beginnings and endings:

bl	ue
gr	oom
st	ew
f	ool
p	use

_____   _____   _____

_____   _____   _____

_____   _____   _____

_____   _____   _____

Practice 7-B: The Ending -s

1 For many words, just add -s.

But, if the word ends with s, x, z, sh, or ch, add -es.

-s	kiss	+	es	➡	kisses
-x	box	+	es	➡	boxes
-z	buzz	+	es	➡	buzzes
-sh	wish	+	es	➡	wishes
-ch	match	+	es	➡	matches

2 Add -s or -es to each word.

cousin _____   peach _____

march _____   guess _____

pass _____   mix _____

suit _____   tune _____

tax _____   buzz _____

move _____   room _____

spoon _____   brush _____

3 If a word ends with a vowel + y, just add -s.   **day + s ➡ days**

If a word ends with a consonant + y, change the y to i. Then add -es.   **cry**
cri + es ➡ cries

Add the right -s ending to each word.

boy _____   family _____

play _____   turkey _____

fly _____   party _____

tray _____   worry _____

baby _____   factory _____

spy _____   valley _____

4 Add the right -s ending to these action words (verbs). Fill in the blanks. Read the sentences.

1. dry   Ray _____ the dishes.

2. miss   She _____ her friends.

3. stay   Luke _____ up late.

4. wax   Jane _____ the car.

5. watch   Bruce _____ TV a lot.

6. shoot   The hunter _____ his gun.

7. rush   Ruth _____ to her office.

8. carry   Hugh _____ a big box.

9. fry   Pete _____ the eggs.

10. coach   Judy _____ our team.

11. chew   My dog _____ on a bone.

12. fix   Mom _____ dinner for us.

13. pray   The nun _____ to God.

14. cash   Louis _____ the check.

15. try   June _____ on the dresses.

16. use   Luther _____ my tools.

17. study   Sue _____ for a test.

18. buy   He _____ a new truck.

5 Nouns are words that name persons, places, or things. Many nouns have the -s ending. Take the ending off these nouns.

ladies _____

glasses _____

keys _____

clues _____

foxes _____

churches _____

stories _____

dishes _____

Practice 7-C: The Ending -ing

1

For many words, including all words that end with y, just add -ing.

work + ing ➡ working
sleep + ing ➡ sleeping
cry + ing ➡ crying
say + ing ➡ saying

For words that end in silent e, drop the e before adding -ing.

giv~~e~~ + ing ➡ giving
argu~~e~~ + ing ➡ arguing

2

Add -ing to these verbs (action words).

buy _____	marry _____
chew _____	dream _____
rest _____	shake _____
cure _____	rescue _____
fry _____	shine _____
use _____	check _____
spray _____	include _____

3

Double the last consonant before adding -ing when a one-syllable word ends in CVC (Consonant-Vowel-Consonant).

$\overset{cvc}{}$
—CVC   grab + b + ing ➡ grabbing
$\overset{cvc}{}$
—CVC   whip + p + ing ➡ whipping

But do *not* double the last consonant if the word ends in VCC, VCCC, or VVC.

$\overset{vcc}{}$
—VCC   spell + ing ➡ spelling
$\overset{vccc}{}$
—VCCC   watch + ing ➡ watching
$\overset{vvc}{}$
—VVC   look + ing ➡ looking

4

Label the last three letters, as in the first word. Add -ing, doubling the last consonant if you have to. Read the words.

$\overset{cvc}{}$
shut   *shutting*   plant _____
hold _____   drop _____
skid _____   load _____
dust _____   light _____
steal _____   slap _____
block _____   beg _____
plug _____   fool _____
catch _____   toast _____
train _____   hit _____

5

Add -ing to these verbs. Fill in the blanks. Read the sentences.

1. nag   His wife keeps _____ him.
2. save   We started _____ our money.
3. greet   He gave us a warm _____.
4. worry   You are _____ too much.
5. swim   Bruce is in the _____ pool.
6. melt   The ice is _____.
7. move   Are they _____ to the city?
8. plan   Judy is _____ a wedding.
9. fight   The army was _____ a war.

6

Take off the ending and write the root word. Read the words.

playing _____
drinking _____
hearing _____
bragging _____
switching _____
stirring _____
believing _____
ruining _____
continuing _____

Practice 7-D: The Ending -y

New word: adjective

1

The ending -y is added to many words to make adjectives (words that describe persons, places, or things).

Just add -y to many words.

rust + y ➡ rusty
creep + y ➡ creepy
chew + y ➡ chewy

For words ending in e, drop the e before adding -y.

eas~~e~~ + y ➡ easy
shad~~e~~ + y ➡ shady
edg~~e~~ + y ➡ edgy

2

Add -y to these words to make adjectives.

shine	_____	tooth	_____
chill	_____	need	_____
juice	_____	breeze	_____
gloom	_____	stick	_____
snow	_____	rose	_____
spice	_____	health	_____
crunch	_____	scare	_____

3

Double the last consonant before adding -y when a one-syllable word ends in CVC (Consonant-Vowel-Consonant).

—CVC $\overset{CVC}{grab}$ + b + y ➡ grabby

—CVC $\overset{CVC}{nip}$ + p + y ➡ nippy

But do *not* double the last consonant if the word ends in VCC, VCCC, or VVC.

—VCC $\overset{VCC}{smell}$ + y ➡ smelly

—VCCC $\overset{VCCC}{itch}$ + y ➡ itchy

—VVC $\overset{VVC}{cheer}$ + y ➡ cheery

4

Label the last three letters, as in the first word. Add -y, doubling the last consonant if you have to. Read the words.

$\overset{VCC}{trick}$ *tricky*   storm _____

mood _____   blur _____

bump _____   room _____

run _____   crab _____

sneak _____   might _____

starch _____   snoop _____

skin _____   curl _____

rain _____   smog _____

nut _____   dirt _____

5

Add -y to these words to make adjectives. Fill in the blanks. Read the sentences.

1. mud   The kitchen floor is _____.

2. wave   Judy has short _____ hair.

3. soap   Wash the dishes in _____ water.

4. fur   She picked up the _____ cat.

5. crisp   We ate _____ fried chicken.

6. flake   This pie has a _____ crust.

7. mold   That bread is getting _____.

8. wealth   His family is very _____.

9. leak   That home has a _____ roof.

6

Take off the ending and write the root word. Read the words.

speedy _____

dusty _____

witty _____

greasy _____

thirsty _____

fussy _____

slimy _____

worthy _____

sunny _____

Practice 7-E: The Endings -ed and -er

1 For words ending in *e*, just add *-d* or *-r*.

smoke + **d** ➡ **smoked**

+ **r** ➡ **smoker**

For most words ending with a consonant + *y*, change the *y* to *i*, and add *-ed* or *-er*.

carry

carri + **ed** ➡ **carried**

carri + **er** ➡ **carrier**

But for words ending with a vowel + *y*, just add *-ed* or *-er*.

play + **ed** ➡ **played**

+ **er** ➡ **player**

2 Add *-ed* to these verbs.

hire _____

stay _____

die _____

try _____

remove _____

pray _____

study _____

rescue _____

Add *-er* to these verbs.

buy _____

rule _____

lose _____

worry _____

spray _____

shave _____

freeze _____

vote _____

3 Double the last consonant before *-ed* or *-er* when a one-syllable word ends in CVC (Consonant-Vowel-Consonant).

—CVC $\overset{cvc}{\text{rob}}$ + **b** + **ed** ➡ **robbed**

rob + **b** + **er** ➡ **robber**

But do not double the last consonant if the word ends in VCC, VCCC, or V VC.

—VCC $\overset{vcc}{\text{rent}}$ + **ed** ➡ **rented**

+ **er** ➡ **renter**

—VCCC $\overset{vccc}{\text{march}}$ + **ed** ➡ **marched**

+ **er** ➡ **marcher**

—VVC $\overset{vvc}{\text{train}}$ + **ed** ➡ **trained**

+ **er** ➡ **trainer**

4 Label the last three letters, as in the first word. Add the endings, doubling the last consonant if you have to.

-ed

$\overset{cvc}{\text{ship}}$ *shipped*

roast _____

tap _____

learn _____

pass _____

brag _____

roar _____

-er

$\overset{vvc}{\text{room}}$ *roomer*

pitch _____

deal _____

build _____

dip _____

camp _____

bat _____

5 Add *-ed* to these verbs and fill in the blanks. Read the sentences.

1. plug   Sue _____ in the lamp.

2. fold   She _____ the clean sheets.

3. mop   Luke _____ up the water.

4. scratch   The cat _____ my hand.

5. cheer   The letter _____ me up.

6. confuse   The signs _____ us.

7. hurry   Ruth _____ to the bus stop.

8. pack   Judy _____ her bags.

6 Take off the ending and write the root word. Read the words.

refused _____

shopper _____

seller _____

tried _____

swimmer _____

tied _____

argued _____

fighter _____

Practice 7-F: The Endings -er and -est

1 The ending *-er* can also be added to adjectives (words that describe nouns).

As an adjective ending, *-er* means "more." It is used to compare *two* nouns.

The ending *-est* means "most." It is used to compare *more than two* nouns.

My watch is <u>cheaper</u> than yours.
His watch is the <u>cheapest</u> of all.

Today is <u>hotter</u> than yesterday.
Sunday was the <u>hottest</u> day this week.

Note: The rules for adding *-est* are the same as for *-er*.

2 Add both *-er* and *-est* to each adjective, as shown.

cool	*cooler, coolest*
sad	_____
easy	_____
flat	_____
pure	_____
weak	_____
slim	_____

thin	_____
angry	_____
warm	_____
true	_____
short	_____
light	_____
sweet	_____

3 Fill in the blank by adding the right ending (*-er* or *-est*) to the adjective. Read the sentences.

1. big   That car is the _____ one on the lot.

2. old   _____ people get sick more often.

3. lucky   Sue is the _____ person I know.

4. fat   Luke is _____ than Louis.

5. safe   Hide the jewels in the _____ place.

6. high   That is the _____ building in the city.

7. dim   The light is getting _____ .

8. dear   Judy is one of my _____ friends.

9. pretty   Ruth is _____ than her sister.

4 Review all of the endings: *-s*, *-ing*, *-y*, *-ed*, *-er*, *-est*.
Drop the endings and write the root words.

trays	_____	wettest	_____	preacher	_____
hairy	_____	happier	_____	churches	_____
losing	_____	leaving	_____	cheating	_____
cried	_____	drafty	_____	funniest	_____
shaky	_____	begged	_____	grinning	_____
server	_____	glasses	_____	excused	_____
setting	_____	redder	_____	drippy	_____
rudest	_____	soaked	_____	sharpest	_____
tasty	_____	hurries	_____	trimmer	_____

Practice 8-A: *oo* = /uu/

1

cook

good

foot

poor

oo

2 Write the letters and say the word.

b	___ ook	g	___ ood
c	___ ook	h	___ ood
h	___ ook	w	___ ood
l	___ ook	st	___ ood
t	___ ook		
sh	___ ook	w	___ ool
br	___ ook		
cr	___ ook	f	___ oot

3 Read the words.

took	hood
hook	stood
crook	good
book	wood
look	
shook	wool
cook	
brook	foot

4 Write the word you hear.

1. _____ 9. _____

2. _____ 10. _____

3. _____ 11. _____

4. _____ 12. _____

5. _____ 13. _____

6. _____ 14. _____

7. _____

8. _____

5 Read the sentences. **Review words:** poor, woods, understood, notebook, become

1. His foot hurt when he stood up.

2. We burn wood in our stove.

3. Look in the cookbook for a good dish.

4. Hang your wool scarf on the hook.

5. The poor man hoped to become rich.

6. The crook took my good jewels.

7. I took a look under the car's hood.

8. A brook runs through the woods.

9. The men stood up and shook hands.

10. It looks like the poor dog cut its foot.

11. Luke never understood that math book.

12. Did Bruce become hooked on drugs?

13. Judy took good notes in her notebook.

14. June's wool coat has a hood.

15. Louis has become a good cook.

16. That pile of wood is one foot high.

6 **Homonyms:** through and threw

He read through the book.

Are you through with my hammer?

I heard the news through a neighbor.

Ruth threw the football to him.

I'll be _____ working at noon.

The children ran _____ the garden.

Louis _____ down the newspaper.

I got help _____ a tutor.

Practice 8-B: Irregular /uu/: *u, ou, o*

1 Read the words.

u	ou	o
bull	could	wolf
full	would	woman
pull	should	
bush		
push		
put		
sure		
lure		

2 Write the word you hear.

1. _____   10. _____
2. _____   11. _____
3. _____   12. _____
4. _____   13. _____
5. _____
6. _____
7. _____
8. _____
9. _____

3 Read the sentences.　　**New word:** cookie　　**Review words:** Bush, sugar, beautiful, hardly, only

1. He pushed the big box, and I pulled it.
2. She could hardly put the book down.
3. That woman should not have pushed me.
4. Luke hoped the lure would catch a fish.
5. Are you sure where to plant this bush?
6. He said he would sell only one bull.
7. Bruce was sure he had seen a wolf.
8. The jar is only half full of cookies.

9. The woman put on a beautiful dress.
10. I'm sure Judy Bush could get me a job.
11. Hardly any sugar cookies were eaten.
12. The yard is full of beautiful bushes.
13. It was so dark he could hardly see.
14. We should buy that beautiful picture.
15. Would you put some sugar on the cookies?
16. Dr. Bush had to pull only one tooth.

4 **Homonyms:** would and wood

She hoped they would visit her.

Would you come with me?

The table is made of wood.

Throw that _____ on the fire.

_____ you like to quit your job?

She said she _____ be home soon.

We need _____ to make paper.

Practice 9-A: *ou* = /ou/ as in *-out, -our, -oud*

1

out
shout
-out

our
hour
-our

proud
-oud

2 Write the letters and say the word.

	out		our
p	___ out	h	___ our
sh	___ out	s	___ our
tr	___ out	fl	___ our
st	___ out	sc	___ our
sc	___ out		
sp	___ out	l	___ oud
sn	___ out	cl	___ oud
spr	___ out	pr	___ oud

3 Read the words.

shout	sour
spout	flour
out	our
snout	scour
trout	hour
pout	
scout	cloud
sprout	proud
stout	loud

4 Write the word you hear.

1. _____   10. _____
2. _____   11. _____
3. _____   12. _____
4. _____   13. _____
5. _____   14. _____
6. _____   15. _____
7. _____   16. _____
8. _____   17. _____
9. _____

5 Read the sentences.   **Review words:** about, without

1. Mix in about one cup of flour.

2. We are proud of our children.

3. He shouted our names out loud.

4. We went trout fishing for two hours.

5. The clouds are dark. Will it rain?

6. What is the little girl pouting about?

7. What did the scout find out?

8. Without sugar, this fruit is too sour.

9. Scour the sink until it is clean.

10. Mr. Bush is short and stout.

11. Our son was proud of the trout he got.

12. We went without speaking for an hour.

13. Our seeds are about to sprout.

14. "That music is too loud!" I shouted.

15. The pig sniffs with his snout.

16. Water came out of the spout.

6 **Homonyms:** our and hour

Did you see our new car?

He will finish in an hour.

We relax during the dinner hour.

What _____ do you start work?

It takes an _____ to read that book.

_____ family is getting bigger.

He tried to steal _____ money.

23

Practice 9-B: *ou = /ou/* as in *-ouse, -oul, -oun, -ouch, -outh*

1

house
-ouse

foul
-oul

noun
-oun

couch
-ouch

south
-outh

2 Write the letters and say the word.

h ___ ouse	c ___ ouch
l ___ ouse	p ___ ouch
m ___ ouse	v ___ ouch
bl ___ ouse	sl ___ ouch
sp ___ ouse	cr ___ ouch
	gr ___ ouch
f ___ oul	
	m ___ outh
n ___ oun	s ___ outh

3 Read the words.

mouse	pouch
blouse	slouch
louse	couch
spouse	grouch
house	vouch
	crouch
foul	
	south
noun	mouth

4 Write the word you hear.

1. _____
2. _____
3. _____
4. _____
5. _____
6. _____
7. _____
8. _____
9. _____
10. _____
11. _____
12. _____
13. _____
14. _____
15. _____

5 Read the sentences.   **Review word:** thousand

1. Judy wore a blue blouse.

2. She put some food in her mouth.

3. We live in a house on the south side.

4. The player got three fouls.

5. He carried the mail in a big pouch.

6. They drove south for a thousand miles.

7. Our cat crouched near the couch.

   He was ready to jump on the mouse.

8. You and your spouse must sign the form.

9. Bruce slouched on the couch.

10. I spent thousands to fix up the house.

11. A noun names a person, place, or thing.

12. We knew there was a mouse in the house.

13. I can vouch for the truth of his story.

14. That grouch is a real louse!

15. What a foul mouth he has!

6 **Homonyms:** do and dew

The lawn was covered with dew.

Do you want to do the work?

They do not like your friend.

We _____ not plan to go.

_____ makes the grass wet.

_____ you have any pets?

They _____ their studying at night.

24

Practice 9-C: *ou* = /ou/ as in -*ound*, -*ount*, -*ounce*, -*ounge*

1

ground

sound

-ound

count

-ount

bounce

-ounce

lounge

-ounge

2   Write the letters and say the word.

b ___ ound		c ___ ount	
f ___ ound		m ___ ount	
h ___ ound			
m ___ ound			ounce
p ___ ound		b ___ ounce	
r ___ ound		p ___ ounce	
s ___ ound			
w ___ ound		l ___ ounge	
gr ___ ound			

3   Read the words.

round	mount
hound	count
wound	
bound	pounce
ground	ounce
found	bounce
pound	
sound	lounge
mound	

4   Write the word you hear.

1. _____ 10. _____
2. _____ 11. _____
3. _____ 12. _____
4. _____ 13. _____
5. _____ 14. _____
6. _____ 15. _____
7. _____
8. _____
9. _____

5   Read the sentences.   **Review words:** around, mountain

1. The man counted out a thousand dollars.
2. Her hound rolled around on the ground.
3. The road wound around the mountain.
4. There are 16 ounces in a pound.
5. She found a friend she can count on.
6. Mount a horse and ride up the mountain.
7. The top I found spins round and round.
8. A loud sound made me bounce out of bed.
9. Give me a pound of ground round.
10. Our team is bound to win.
11. Pound in the nail to mount the picture.
12. We found a couch to put in the lounge.
13. My hound dug up the ground around here.
14. Our cat pounced on a mouse.
15. The pitcher stood on the mound.
16. I wound my clock, but it made no sound.

6   Two ways to say <u>wound</u>:
    OU = /oo/ and /ou/

/oo/   The bullet <u>wounded</u> him.
      He had some bad <u>wounds</u>.
/ou/   I <u>wound</u> the alarm clock.

_/___/ The thread is <u>wound</u> around the spool.

_/___/ The doctor stitched up her <u>wound</u>.

_/___/ Hugh was <u>wounded</u> in the fight.

_/___/ Every night she <u>wound</u> her watch.

Practice 10-A: *ow* = /ou/ as in *-ow, -owl, -owd*

1

how

cow

-ow

growl

-owl

crowd

-owd

2 Write the letters and say the word.

b _____ ow   owl

c _____ ow   f _____ owl

h _____ ow   h _____ owl

n _____ ow   gr _____ owl

s _____ ow   pr _____ owl

v _____ ow

ch _____ ow

br _____ ow

pl _____ ow   cr _____ owd

3 Read the words.

now   howl

chow   prowl

bow   owl

plow   fowl

cow   growl

how

brow

vow

sow   crowd

4 Write the word you hear.

1. _____   10. _____

2. _____   11. _____

3. _____   12. _____

4. _____   13. _____

5. _____   14. _____

6. _____   15. _____

7. _____

8. _____

9. _____

5 Read the sentences.   **New word:** allow   **Review words:** Howard, won't

1. How much milk does that cow give?

2. He took a bow as the crowd cheered.

3. A man was prowling around our house.

  Our dog growled at him.

4. At night in the woods, the owl hoots.

  And the wolf howls at the moon.

5. We raise sows and chickens on the farm.

6. Howard won't allow us to plow the field.

7. Howard wiped the sweat from his brow.

8. No smoking is allowed here now.

9. That dog won't stop howling.

10. Howard hunts ducks and other fowl.

11. How much chow will the cowboys eat?

12. Howard and Sue spoke their vows.

13. We plowed our way through the crowd.

14. Why won't he allow us to leave now?

6 Two ways to say <u>bow</u>:

  OW = /ō/ or /ou/

/ō/   Tie the shoelaces in a <u>bow</u>.

  Use this <u>bow</u> to play the violin.

  I shot the arrows with my <u>bow</u>.

/ou/   She <u>bowed</u> as the audience clapped.

  We sat in the <u>bow</u> of the ship.

/___/   Put a new string on this <u>bow</u>.

/___/   Move to the <u>bow</u> of the boat.

/___/   He has on a red <u>bow</u> tie.

/___/   The singer took a <u>bow</u>.

Practice 10-B: *ow = /ou/* **as in** *-own, -ower, -owel*

1

town

-own

flower

-ower

towel

-owel

2 Write the letters and say the word.

d _____ own	p _____ ower
g _____ own	t _____ ower
t _____ own	sh _____ ower
cl _____ own	fl _____ ower
br _____ own	
cr _____ own	
dr _____ own	t _____ owel
fr _____ own	v _____ owel

3 Read the words.

town	shower
crown	power
down	flower
frown	tower
clown	
drown	
gown	vowel
brown	towel

4 Write the word you hear.

1. _____   9. _____
2. _____   10. _____
3. _____   11. _____
4. _____   12. _____
5. _____   13. _____
6. _____   14. _____
7. _____
8. _____

5 Read the sentences. **Review words:** Howard, Brown, against, county, council, court, fair

1. Use this towel after your shower.

2. Mr. Brown drowned in that lake.

3. The queen wore a blue gown and a crown.

4. The clown only smiles. He never frowns.

5. The town council voted against my plan.

6. Sue wrote down the short vowel words.

7. The rain shower watered my flowers.

8. Did you buy that brown suit downtown?

9. Howard Brown is a county court judge.

10. The city council has a lot of power.

11. Set the brown towel down there.

12. I spoke against building a power plant.

13. The church has a high tower with bells.

14. We'll see clowns at the county fair.

15. "My grades are down," he said, frowning.

16. Howard runs the flower shop in town.

6 **Confusing words:** flower and flour

Use whole wheat <u>flour</u> to make the bread.

Roses are beautiful <u>flowers</u>.

That plant <u>flowers</u> in late fall.

I need _____ to make cookies.

Add some milk to the _____ mix.

This tree will _____ in the spring.

We have a lovely _____ garden.

Practice 11-A: Review of /uu/ and /ou/

1 Look at the picture and say the word. Then write the word.

_____	_____	_____

_____	_____	_____

2 Use these words to fill in the blanks:

wool	flour	sure	stood
house	growl	took	crowd

1. Sue needs _____ and sugar to make cookies.

2. Many people in the _____ began to shout.

3. Judy put on a blue blouse and a brown _____ skirt.

4. We should plant bushes and flowers around our _____.

5. I am _____ Mrs. Brown is the best cook in town.

6. It _____ Howard an hour to look through the book.

7. Our dog would _____ when he heard a sound.

8. The proud woman _____ up and took a bow.

3 Circle all the words that are the same as the first one.

shout	shut	shout	shoot	stout	south	shout	shot
now	now	won	mow	now	how	new	row
push	posh	bush	push	shop	gush	bush	push
foot	toot	foot	feet	loot	foot	fort	boot
flour	flour	four	floor	flour	foul	flower	flour

4 Make at least 12 words with these beginnings and endings:

br	ound	_____	_____	_____
h	ook	_____	_____	_____
p	ow	_____	_____	_____
c	ouch	_____	_____	_____
b	own	_____	_____	_____

Practice 11-B: The Ending -*ly*

1 Just add -*ly* to most words, including those with final *l* or silent *e*. Add -*ly* to these nouns to make adjectives that describe a person, place, or thing.

love   a _lovely_ woman

order   an _____ class

brother   _____ love

wool   a _____ coat

cost   a _____ mistake

friend   a _____ face

heaven   a _____ place

2 Add -*ly* to these words to describe *how often* something happens.

week   a _____ TV show

year   a _____ tax

month   a _____ bill

night   the _____ news

quarter   a _____ checkup

hour   an _____ wage

3 Add -*ly* to these adjectives to make words that describe *how* something is done.

proud   He spoke _____ of his son.

near   Sue _____ quit her job.

poor   He did _____ on the test.

slow   I drove _____ through town.

loose   This belt fits _____.

rude   She spoke _____ to us.

safe   Did they arrive _____?

4 Add -*ly* to these adjectives to make words that describe *how* something is done.

fair _____   brave _____

pure _____   quick _____

loud _____   stupid _____

sad _____   sharp _____

deep _____   cruel _____

firm _____   smooth _____

cool _____   strange _____

most _____   slight _____

wild _____   close _____

5 To add -*ly* to a word that ends with *y*, change the *y* to *i* and add -*ly*.

gay   **happy**
gai + ly ➡ **gaily**   **happi** + ly ➡ **happily**

easy   The job can be _____ done.

greedy   We ate the food _____.

lucky   _____, no one was hurt.

day   I read the _____ paper.

angry   Judy yelled at us _____.

sleepy   He opened his eyes _____.

6 Take off the -*ly* ending.

really _____

heavily _____

securely _____

daily _____

freely _____

surely _____

mainly _____

rarely _____

steadily _____

29

Practice 12-A: *aw* = /aw/

1

saw

law

claw

-aw

2 Write the letters and say the word.

j ——— aw   dr ——— aw

l ——— aw   str ——— aw

r ——— aw

p ——— aw

s ——— aw

th ——— aw

cl ——— aw

fl ——— aw

sl ——— aw

3 Read the words.

saw   law

draw   claw

jaw

slaw

paw

flaw

raw

thaw

straw

4 Write the word you hear.

1. _____   10. _____

2. _____   11. _____

3. _____

4. _____

5. _____

6. _____

7. _____

8. _____

9. _____

5 Read the sentences.   **Review words:** awful, awfully, Shaw, dog, Jerry

1. The dog hurt its paw.

2. Jerry fixed some slaw for lunch.

3. Mr. Shaw put on his straw hat.

4. My cat has awfully sharp claws.

5. Thaw the raw meat. Then cook it.

6. Speeding is against the law.

7. We saw that movie. It was awful!

8. Draw the water up through the straw.

9. I saw that the glass had a flaw in it.

10. Jerry put the saw in the tool shed.

11. My dog clawed at the door to get in.

12. That movie will draw a large crowd.

13. Jerry Shaw plans to study law.

14. Have you ever eaten raw fish?

15. My tooth hurts. My jaw is awfully sore.

16. The pictures she draws look awful.

6 **Homonyms:** <u>fowl</u> and <u>foul</u>

He raises hens and other <u>fowl</u>.

Jerry hit a <u>foul</u> ball.

That player got a <u>foul</u>.

Her language is <u>foul</u>.

Our team has three _____s.

What a _____ crime that was!

This book tells how to cook _____.

Don't listen to his _____ speech.

Practice 12-B: *aw* = /aw/ as in -*awn*, -*awk*, -*awl*

1

lawn
crawl
hawk
-aw

2 Write the letters and say the word.

d ____ awn	b ____ awl
f ____ awn	sh ____ awl
l ____ awn	br ____ awl
p ____ awn	cr ____ awl
y ____ awn	dr ____ awl
dr ____ awn	spr ____ awl
h ____ awk	
squ ____ awk	

3 Read the words.

lawn	crawl
yawn	bawl
drawn	drawl
pawn	sprawl
fawn	brawl
dawn	shawl
squawk	
hawk	

4 Write the word you hear.

1. _____
2. _____
3. _____
4. _____
5. _____
6. _____
7. _____
8. _____
9. _____
10. _____
11. _____
12. _____
13. _____
14. _____

5 Read the sentences.   **Review words:** Dawson, sorry, couldn't

1. The baby couldn't crawl very far.
2. I was sorry I had to pawn my jewels.
3. Judy Dawson heard her baby bawling.
4. I'm sorry my dog dug up your lawn.
5. She wore a wool shawl over her head.
6. The hawk swooped down on the hen.
   The hen gave a loud squawk.
7. At dawn Jerry woke up with a yawn.

8. These pictures were drawn by Ed Dawson.
9. We saw a fawn in the woods.
10. The men in the bar got into a brawl.
11. Jerry sprawled in the big chair.
12. We couldn't rid our lawn of weeds.
13. He yawned and crawled into bed.
14. I had drawn my money out of the bank.
15. She spoke slowly, with a drawl.

6 **Homonyms:** Circle the right word.

1. Judy painted the car (blew, blue).
2. Did you (root, route) for our team?
3. None of us (new, knew) her name.
4. I was (to, too) tired to go (to, too) work.
5. The lawn is covered with (do, dew).
6. Grease and (flour, flower) the pan.
7. He got sick and (threw, through) up.
8. We didn't think he (wood, would) win.

31

Practice 12-C: *au* = /aw/

1

haul
sauce
fault
au

2 Read the words.

haul	cause	fraud
maul	pause	
Paul	because	author
Paula		
	gauze	caution
fault		
vault	haunt	August
	launch	
sauce	laundry	auto

3 Write the word you hear.

1. _____ 10. _____

2. _____ 11. _____

3. _____ 12. _____

4. _____ 13. _____

5. _____ 14. _____

6. _____ 15. _____

7. _____ 16. _____

8. _____ 17. _____

9. _____ 18. _____

4 Read the sentences. **New words:** he's, she's **Review words:** automobile, accident, spaceship

1. Paula put the money in the bank vault.

2. He says he's a doctor, but he's a fraud.

3. That auto accident was Paul's fault!

   He caused it by not using caution.

4. She's making barbeque sauce for ribs.

5. The author wrote about a haunted house.

6. In August, they will launch a spaceship.

7. Paul's truck hauls laundry into town.

8. Did the bear maul that man?

9. New automobiles go on sale in August.

10. She's angry because he's late.

11. Laundry soap got that sauce stain out.

12. Paula hauled the dirt in a dump truck.

13. I paused because I saw a caution sign.

14. She has only one fault—she's greedy!

15. A nurse put a gauze pad over the cut.

5 Fill in *aw* or *au* to make words for the sentences, as in number 1.

1. The baby cr a w ls on the floor.

2. P ___ l has dr ___ n these pictures.

3. Put the jewels in the v ___ lt.

4. A ghost h ___ nts that house.

5. When can you mow the l ___ n?

6. The h ___ k has sharp cl ___ s.

7. What was the c ___ se of the accident?

8. I s ___ the sun come up at d ___ n.

Practice 13-A: *all* = /awl/

1

ball
fall
small
-all

2 Write the letters and say the word.

	all
b	___ all
c	___ all
f	___ all
h	___ all
t	___ all
w	___ all
sm	___ all
st	___ all

3 Read the words.

tall
call
all
small
wall
ball
stall
hall
fall

4 Write the word you hear.

1. _____
2. _____
3. _____
4. _____
5. _____
6. _____
7. _____
8. _____
9. _____

5 Read the sentences.

Review words: basketball, baseball, football, winter, season, August, February, September, November, December

1. We all met in the room down the hall.
2. This stall is too small for my horse.
3. "Play ball!" the coach called out.
4. Did the picture fall off the wall?
5. Our football season ends in November.
6. In December I moved into a small house.
7. All the basketball players are tall.
8. Winter and fall are the seasons I love!
9. The baseball player ran into the wall.
10. The Dawsons call their baby boy Jerry.
11. I start school this fall in September.
12. We rented a big hall for the ball.
13. If your car stalls, call a tow truck.
14. Our tree is small, just six feet tall.
15. We saw the February 1 basketball game.
16. All work was stalled until August.

6 **Homonyms:** ball and bawl

The ball player has one ball and two strikes.

The child played with a rubber ball.

They danced together at the ball.

I told my son to stop his bawling.

I tried to catch the _____.

The hungry child started to _____.

She wore a new dress to the _____.

Our _____ team wins every game.

Practice 13-B: *a* = /aw/

1

salt
false
talk
wash

a

2 Write the letters and say the word.

b	___ ald	w	___ alk
sc	___ ald	t	___ alk
		ch	___ alk
s	___ alt	st	___ alk
h	___ alt		
m	___ alt		
W	___ alt		
		w	___ ash
f	___ alse	squ	___ ash

3 Read the words.

scald	chalk
bald	talk
	stalk
Walt	walk
halt	
salt	
malt	
	wash
false	squash

4 Write the word you hear.

1. _____   10. _____

2. _____   11. _____

3. _____   12. _____

4. _____   13. _____

5. _____

6. _____

7. _____

8. _____

9. _____

5 Read the sentences.   **New words:** always, almost   **Review words:** also, water

1. Walt is almost bald.

2. Add some salt to the squash.

3. She is always willing to talk to me.

4. Does Walt have false teeth?

5. I wrote on the board with white chalk.

6. Walt had a sandwich and also a malt.

7. Always wash your hands before meals.

8. The corn grows on tall stalks.

9. Jerry talked for almost an hour.

10. The bald man is wearing a wig.

11. Walt walked almost four miles.

12. Buy some salt and also some sugar.

13. She is always spreading false stories.

14. The wash water is scalding hot.

15. The bread got squashed in that bag.

16. The army halted after walking an hour.

6 **Homonyms:** hall and haul

I walked down the long hall.

A crowd gathered in the large hall.

Haul that garbage away.

Big trucks _____ the heavy loads.

_____ the boxes to the factory.

The office is in the town _____.

The bedroom is down the _____.

Practice 14-A: *-ought, -aught* = /awt/

1

bought
thought
-ought

caught
-aught

2 Write the letters and say the word.

	ought	c	___ aught
b	___ ought	t	___ aught
f	___ ought		
s	___ ought		
th	___ ought		
br	___ ought		

3 Read the words.

thought	taught
fought	caught
brought	
ought	daughter
sought	
bought	naughty

4 Write the word you hear.

1. _____   10. _____
2. _____
3. _____
4. _____
5. _____
6. _____
7. _____
8. _____
9. _____

5 Read the sentences.   **Review words:** war, American, between, summer, ticket, country

1. He brought us some fish he had caught.
2. That naughty girl ought to be scolded.
3. Many Americans fought in that war.
4. I was brought up in another country.
5. My daughter taught in summer school.
6. I thought you had bought her a gift.
7. My daughter Paula can be very naughty.
8. Paul sought a job in the city.
9. Paula bought a new summer dress.
10. I caught that naughty boy telling lies.
11. Many Americans sought peace, not war.
12. I taught my daughter how to cook.
13. A war was fought between two countries.
14. I bought a ticket and caught the plane.
15. We thought he ought to quit his job.
16. He taught class between two and four.

6 Fill in *all*, *al*, or *aul* to make words for the sentences, as in number 1.

1. **Paul** is not very **tall** .
2. Add some s_____t to the stew.
3. Did she f_____ on the steps?
4. W_____t ran down the h_____ .
5. Please h_____ that junk away.
6. He has so many f_____ts .
7. Jerry is not b_____d yet.
8. Those stories are f_____se , not true.

35

Practice 14-B: Irregular /aw/: o as in -og, -ong, -onk, -oth

1

dog
-og

honk
-onk

song
-ong

cloth
-oth

2 Write the letters and say the word.

d ____ og   l ____ ong

f ____ og   s ____ ong

h ____ og   g ____ ong

l ____ og   wr ____ ong

fr ____ og   str ____ ong

m ____ oth

cl ____ oth

h ____ onk   br ____ oth

3 Read the words.

hog   song

fog   wrong

log   long

frog   strong

dog   gong

broth

moth

honk   cloth

4 Write the word you hear.

1. _____   10. _____

2. _____   11. _____

3. _____   12. _____

4. _____   13. _____

5. _____   14. _____

6. _____

7. _____

8. _____

9. _____

5 Read the sentences.   **New words:** belong, gone   **Review word:** along

1. That big, strong dog belongs to us.

2. Paul sang the song along with us.

3. He cooked the broth for a long time.

4. The farmer raises hogs for food.

5. I drove along slowly through the fog.

6. The moths ate holes in the cloth.

7. The frog jumped up on the log.

8. The strong man chopped up the logs.

9. She has gone away on a long trip.

10. He rang the gong to call us to dinner.

11. The money that belongs to us is gone.

    It was wrong for him to steal it.

12. A dog ran out. The driver honked at it.

13. By morning the fog was gone.

14. You sang that song all wrong!

15. That cloth belongs in my sewing basket.

6 Fill in *aught* or *ought* to make words for the sentences, as in number 1.

1. Walt t _aught_ ____ in high school.

2. They f _____ and died in the war.

3. Dad s _____ a better job.

4. Jerry c _____ the football.

5. Paula br _____ friends to the party.

6. I c _____ him cheating.

7. We th _____ you were sick.

8. Paul b _____ a new car.

36

Practice 14-C: Irregular /aw/: *o* as in *-oss, -ost, -off, -oft*

1

boss

-oss

cost

-ost

off

soft

-oft

2 Write the letters and say the word.

b	_____ oss	c	_____ ost
l	_____ oss	l	_____ ost
m	_____ oss	fr	_____ ost
R	_____ oss		
t	_____ oss		off
cr	_____ oss		
gl	_____ oss	l	_____ oft
		s	_____ oft

3 Read the words.

loss	lost
moss	frost
cross	cost
gloss	
boss	off
toss	
Ross	soft
	loft

4 Write the word you hear.

1. _____
2. _____
3. _____
4. _____
5. _____
6. _____
7. _____
8. _____
9. _____
10. _____
11. _____
12. _____
13. _____

5 Read the sentences.   **New word:** offer

Review words: often, across, office, officer, coffee, $ (dollar)

1. Cross those names off the list.

2. Did the boss offer you a raise?

3. We sat in the office drinking coffee.

4. Soft, green moss grows on the trees.

5. This loft is full of hay.

6. Ross often lost the keys to the office.

7. We tossed the ball across the field.

8. The loss from the fire cost us $10,000.

9. Ross offered to look for my lost dog.

10. The officer helped us cross the street.

11. Ross scraped the frost off the windows.

12. He lay across the big soft bed.

13. The gold cross that I bought cost $100.

14. Did she offer to frost the cake?

15. My boss often takes long coffee breaks.

16. Wax the car to give it a nice gloss.

6 **Homonyms:** Circle the right word.

1. Jerry read (threw, through) the newspaper.

2. Was that a (foul, fowl) ball?

3. Those people (new, knew) my parents.

4. (Our, Hour) family is taking a trip.

5. We stopped when he (blue, blew) the whistle.

6. Can you hear the baby (ball, bawl)?

7. I can (do, due) the work in one hour.

8. The students walked down the (hall, haul).

Practice 15-A: *oy* = /oy/

1

boy
enjoy
employ
-oy

2 Read the words.

boy	loyal	employ
joy	royal	employer
Joy		employee
Roy	annoy	employment
toy	enjoy	unemployed
	destroy	unemployment

3 Write the word you hear.

1. _____   10. _____
2. _____   11. _____
3. _____   12. _____
4. _____   13. _____
5. _____   14. _____
6. _____   15. _____
7. _____   16. _____
8. _____
9. _____

4 Read the sentences.   **Review words:** Joyce, during, almost, always

1. Roy's new baby boy is a joy to him.
2. Joyce is a loyal employee.
3. I was annoyed when he lost his toy.
4. My unemployment almost destroyed me.
5. We employ more people during the fall.
6. Joyce has made a royal feast for us.
7. Roy's little boy enjoys those toys.
8. Joy's employer always annoys her.
9. Did the royal family enjoy their visit?
10. Many boys are hoping for employment.
11. That city was destroyed during the war.
12. Joy was loyal to her friend Roy.
13. That employer hires unemployed women.
14. Sometimes Joyce's students annoy her.
    But teaching them always gives her joy.
15. He played with toys for almost an hour.

5 **Homonyms:** Circle the right word.

1. Did they (hall, haul) the trash away?
2. I'm going to the zoo, (to, too).
3. She picked a pretty pink (flower, flour).
4. The players like their (new, knew) coach.
5. The rent is (do, due) on July 1.
6. Are you (threw, through) with your work?
7. Use this (wood, would) to make a desk.
8. A plant gets water through its (roots, routes).

Practice 15-B: *oi* = /oy/

1

oil
point
voice
oi

2 Read the words.

oil	coin	voice
boil	join	choice
coil		
foil	joint	noise
soil	point	poise
broil	appoint	
spoil	disappoint	hoist
		moist
poison	avoid	

3 Write the word you hear.

1. _____	10. _____	19. _____
2. _____	11. _____	20. _____
3. _____	12. _____	21. _____
4. _____	13. _____	
5. _____	14. _____	
6. _____	15. _____	
7. _____	16. _____	
8. _____	17. _____	
9. _____	18. _____	

4 Read the sentences. **New word:** likely **Review words:** easy, won, we're, isn't

1. Broil the chicken or fry it in oil.

2. We're planting the seeds in moist soil.

3. This poison kills rats and mice.

4. A loud voice was heard over the noise.

5. Isn't that soup likely to boil over?

6. We're disappointed you didn't join us.

7. The coiled snake is likely to strike.

8. I pointed out many old coins.

9. The meat covered with foil is spoiled.

10. His finger is out of joint.

11. He will appoint the man of our choice.

12. It wasn't easy, but I won by one point.

13. Roy's voice shook. He lost his poise.

14. My shirt was soiled with oil stains.

15. It isn't easy to hoist up that flag.

16. Her son is so spoiled that I avoid him.

5 **Homonyms:** Circle the right word.

1. I'll see you during lunch (our, hour).

2. What can I (do, dew) to help?

3. June caught the bouncing (ball, bawl).

4. (Wood, Would) you like some coffee?

5. Cook that (fowl, foul) in a large pan.

6. I (threw, through) the ball to Paul.

7. A strong wind (blue, blew).

8. Take this (root, route) out of the city.

39

Practice 16-A: Review of /aw/ and /oy/

1 Look at the picture and say the word. Then write the word.

_____   _____   _____

_____   _____   _____

2 Use these words to fill in the blanks:

soil   caught   hall   crawl   enjoy   walks   strong   sauce

1. Did Walt _____ playing football last fall?

2. Paula sang the song with a loud, _____ voice.

3. Joyce bought some slaw, barbeque _____, salt, and coffee at the store.

4. Ross is a tall, bald man who _____ with a limp.

5. The dog hurt its paw and could hardly _____.

6. The boss fired the employees because they were _____ stealing.

7. This laundry soap will get the oil stains and _____ out of that cloth.

8. Roy has the small office at the end of the _____.

3 Circle all the words that are the same as the first one.

hall	hall	halt	ball	wall	hall	haul	hell
avoid	void	avoid	avid	avoid	devoid	voice	avid
dawn	down	wand	dawn	pawn	lawn	drawn	dawn
lost	slot	lost	loss	cost	lots	lost	last
song	son	sang	song	strong	song	sung	smog

4 Make at least 14 words with these beginnings and endings:

t	all	_____	_____	_____
b	ought	_____	_____	_____
f	oss	_____	_____	_____
br	oil	_____	_____	_____
s	oy	_____	_____	_____

Practice 16-B: Irregular Spellings: *o* and *oo* = /u/

1

one
come
some
mother
brother
o
blood
oo

2 Read the words.

none	other	love	among
done	another	lovely	won
does	mother	shove	wonder
son	brother	glove	wonderful
ton	nothing	cover	
month	become	oven	blood
once	money	dozen	flood

3 Write the word you hear.

1. _____   8. _____   15. _____

2. _____   9. _____   16. _____

3. _____   10. _____   17. _____

4. _____   11. _____   18. _____

5. _____   12. _____   19. _____

6. _____   13. _____   20. _____

7. _____   14. _____   21. _____

4 Read the sentences.

1. My son comes to visit once a month.

2. He sent one dozen roses to his mother.

3. Are the cookies in the oven done yet?

4. She has become a wonderful teacher.

5. My son won some money on a bet.

6. Roy does paint lovely pictures.

7. Nothing can be done to stop the flood.

8. I wear gloves when I clean the oven.

9. One brother shoved the other one.

10. He wonders if he can get another job.

11. None of the trucks weighs over ten tons.

12. Her brother loves to spend money.

13. For months she worked among the poor.

14. None of the others would come with me.

15. My son's shirt was covered with blood.

16. Does she plan to become a doctor?

17. We love to hear her wonderful voice!

18. Mother will visit us some other time.

5 Homonyms: won and one

Two can go, but one must stay.

He helps the ones who try.

She won the first prize.

Joy _____ the race.

No _____ said he _____ .

Which team _____ the game?

That book is a hard _____ .

Our family has _____ car.

41

Practice 16-C: Irregular Spellings: *a* = /o/

1

want
watch
water

a

2 Read the words.

want	wallet	swan
watch	waffle	swap
water		swat
watt		swamp
wasp		swallow
wand		squad
wander	yacht	squat

3 Write the word you hear.

1. _____ 8. _____ 15. _____

2. _____ 9. _____ 16. _____

3. _____ 10. _____ 17. _____

4. _____ 11. _____

5. _____ 12. _____

6. _____ 13. _____

7. _____ 14. _____

4 Read the sentences. **New words:** couple, double **Review word:** trouble

1. I want to watch TV for a couple hours.

2. Joyce tried to swat the wasp.

3. He chewed the waffle and swallowed it.

4. What happens when he waves his wand?

5. We want the team to make a double play.

6. They were squatting around the fire.

7. I don't want my children to wander off.

8. The lamp uses a couple of 100-watt lights.

9. A swat on the head made him see double.

10. They watched a swan swim on the lake.

11. He got in trouble for stealing a wallet.

12. The football squad ran out on the field.

13. He paid us double to clean the yacht.

14. I'll swap my watch for your wallet.

15. A couple of kids wandered into the swamp.

16. She yelled when the wasp stung her.

17. The police squad had trouble with gangs.

18. Swallow this pill with some water.

5 Homonyms: <u>son</u> and <u>sun</u>

Roy is my oldest <u>son</u>.

The <u>sun</u> shone brightly.

I have just one _____ .

His _____ plays on the team.

The _____ can burn your skin.

Her _____ is in trouble.

We watch the _____ come up.

The _____ gives heat and light.

Practice 16-D: Vowel + _rr_

1

arr		**err**		**irr**	**orr**		**urr**
marry	carrot	berry	terrify	mirror	correct	sorry	purr
carry	parrot	ferry	terrier	irritate	corral	sorrow	hurry
Harry	marriage	merry	territory	irrigate	horrid	borrow	furry
Larry	embarrass	Terry	errand		horror	tomorrow	blurry
arrow		cherry	strawberry		horrible		current
narrow	quarrel	error			horrify		surround
sparrow	warrant	terror					surrender
barrel	Warren	terrible	interrupt	squirrel		worry	hurricane

---

2 Read the sentences.   **Review words:** Jerry, starry

1. Joyce and Larry had many quarrels during their marriage.

2. Jerry dug narrow ditches to irrigate his land.

3. Can I borrow your car to run some errands tomorrow?

4. The terrier chased the squirrel across the lawn.

5. Would you like carrot cake or cherry pie after dinner?

6. Don't worry about that error. I'll correct it in a hurry.

7. News of the horrible hurricane filled us with sorrow.

8. Armies surrounded the territory, forcing us to surrender.

9. What are Harry's current plans? Will he marry Paula?

10. A large furry cat pounced on the sparrow.

11. This strawberry jam that Harry made is terrific!

12. Police are carrying a warrant to search Terry's house.

13. Warren put a small mirror in the parrot's cage.

14. When Jerry interrupts me, it irritates me.

15. The trash in that barrel smells horrid!

16. I'm sorry we embarrassed you. I feel terrible.

17. We rode on the ferry, looking up at the starry sky.

18. Those horror movies terrify Warren's children.

Practice 16-E: The Endings -ful and -less   New word: reply
Review word: arrest

1 Just add -ful or -less to most words.

sin   + ful ➡ sinful
sleeve + less ➡ sleeveless

For words that end with a consonant + y, change the y to i and add -ful or -less.

beauty
beauti + ful ➡ beautiful

plenty
plenti + ful ➡ plentiful

penny
penni + less ➡ penniless

mercy
merci + less ➡ merciless

2 Add -ful to these words to tell the amount needed to fill something.

cup	a _cupful_	of coffee
spoon	a _____	of sugar
house	a _____	of guests
hand	a _____	of dirt
mouth	a _____	of food
room	a _____	of people
box	a _____	of books
glass	a _____	of milk

3 Add -ful to these nouns to make adjectives. The ending -ful means "full of" or "with."

care	_careful_	plans
cheer	a _____	smile
help	a _____	friend
wonder	_____	books
beauty	a _____	face
play	a _____	puppy
duty	a _____	son
force	a _____	reply
law	a _____	arrest

4 Add -less to these nouns to make adjectives. The ending -less means "without" or "not having."

home	a _homeless_	family
sleep	_____	nights
worth	a _____	check
seed	_____	grapes
sugar	_____	gum
job	a _____	worker
stain	_____	steel
sense	a _____	reply

5 Add -ful and -less to each word, as shown.

use	_useful, useless_
thought	_____
power	_____
harm	_____
pain	_____
taste	_____
hope	_____
fear	_____
thank	_____

6 Add -ly to these -ful and -less words to describe how things can be done.

truthful	reply	_truthfully_
skillful	work	_____
peaceful	rest	_____
faithful	serve	_____
graceful	dance	_____
helpless	watch	_____
restless	sleep	_____
careless	act	_____

44

Practice 16-F: The Endings -*ment* and -*ness*   Review word: advertise

1 Add -*ment* to each verb to make a noun. The ending -*ment* means "the result or condition of being."

appoint	doctor's *appointment*
move	slow _____
retire	early _____
pay	a down _____
employ	steady _____
treat	fair _____
enjoy	great _____
ship	large _____
improve	real _____
state	a true _____
agree	no _____
disappoint	big _____
advertise	TV _____

A few words drop the final *e* before -*ment*. Drop the *e* and add -*ment* to these words.

| judge | poor _____ |
| argue | loud _____ |

2 Add -*ness* to each adjective to make a noun. The ending -*ness* means "a state of being."

sick	_____
neat	_____
bald	_____
fresh	_____
thick	_____
sad	_____
full	_____
loud	_____
cool	_____
kind	_____
weak	_____
sore	_____
soft	_____
bright	_____
fit	_____
sweet	_____
deaf	_____

3 Use these -*ness* words to fill in the blank.

| blindness | fairness | illness | rudeness |
| darkness | goodness | ripeness | stiffness |

1. Her _____ makes people angry.

2. Paul sees _____ in every person.

3. Check that fruit for _____.

4. An accident caused Larry's _____.

5. The judge is known for his _____.

6. The ball player felt a _____ in his arm.

7. I can't see in this _____.

8. Howard died after a long _____.

4 To add -*ness* to most words that end with a consonant + *y*, change the *y* to *i* and add -*ness*. Study the example. Then add -*ness* to the words below.

lovely
loveli + **ness** ➡ **loveliness**

lazy	_____
lonely	_____
friendly	_____
happy	_____
naughty	_____

45

Practice 17-A: Two Sounds for *s*: /s/ and /z/

1

When *s* is at the beginning of a word,	When a word has *ss*,	When *s* is at the end of a word,	When the *-s* ending is added to words ending with the sounds /p/, /t/, /k/, or /f/, *s* = /s/. Otherwise, *s* = /z/.

s = /s/		**ss = /s/**	**s = /s/**	**s = /z/**	**-s = /s/**		**-s = /z/**	
said	soda	miss	us	is	helps	jobs	farms
smile	silent	lesson	bus	his	stops	beds	pages
stir	support	across	this	as	looks	dogs	faces
soft	social	discuss	yes	has	meets	loves	trees
spring	security	depress	gas	was	cuffs	calls	laws
sorry	Saturday	business			laughs	hears	knows

2 Read the sentences. Above each underlined *s* or *ss*, write *s* or *z* to show which sound it has, as shown in number 1.

Review words: above, wouldn't, ago, classroom, swim, salt, stir

1. He spoke in a soft voice. Then he was silent.

2. That summer school teacher has the classroom above ours.

3. His only support is Social Security.

4. She always smiles, even when she gets depressed.

5. Roy says he has six apple trees in his yard.

6. Your bus stops at that corner. Don't miss it.

7. My son looks both ways before he goes across the street.

8. The boss wouldn't discuss his business plans with us.

9. She loves to go to movies with us on Saturdays.

10. We swim during the spring and summer months.

11. The teacher said to read the next six pages of lesson 4.

12. Steve laughs at the funny faces of the clowns.

13. Hugh writes down his address and Social Security number.

14. Stir some salt and baking soda into this mix.

15. He hears that the new business will offer lots of jobs.

16. He knows he broke the tax laws, and he is sorry.

17. Wouldn't you like some hot dogs and soda pop?

18. Yes, I paid the gas bill seven days ago.

19. Sue calls every Saturday and talks for hours.

20. Joyce helps out in the classroom as much as she can.

Practice 17-B: Final *s* = /s/

1 s = /s/

at the end of words of more than one syllable.

atlas	tennis	curious
bonus	arthritis	furious
focus		serious
virus	famous	previous
cactus	jealous	humorous
campus	nervous	dangerous
crisis	joyous	marvelous

2 Write the word you hear.

1. _____   8. _____   15. _____

2. _____   9. _____   16. _____

3. _____   10. _____   17. _____

4. _____   11. _____   18. _____

5. _____   12. _____   19. _____

6. _____   13. _____   20. _____

7. _____   14. _____

3 Read the sentences.   **Review word:** university

1. The news story will focus on the crisis in the cities.

2. Doctors are curious about how that virus causes disease.

3. He was jealous of the workers who got a bonus.

4. It's dangerous to walk across the campus alone at night.

5. That author is famous for her humorous books.

6. Serious crime has gone up since the previous year.

7. The players always get nervous before a tennis match.

8. She sang a joyous song. She has such a marvelous voice!

9. A cactus plant does not need much water.

10. He was curious about my previous job at the university.

11. She stopped playing tennis when her arthritis got worse.

12. We found maps of our state in the U.S. atlas.

13. I was nervous about taking on such a dangerous job.

14. Roy was furious when his car was stolen.

15. Ann was jealous of the famous movie star.

16. Many students on campus are sick with a flu virus.

17. Our state university is facing a serious money crisis.

18. He thought I was being humorous, but I was serious.

Practice 17-C: Two Sounds for _s_ in the Middle of Words: /s/ and /z/

1

When _s_ is between vowels,	When _s_ comes before the sounds /p/, /t/, or /k/	When _s_ comes before other consonant sounds,
s = /z/	**s = /s/**	**s = /z/**

visit	easy	deposit	aspirin	desk	interest	husband
cousin	busy	closet	hospital	east	against	Tuesday
music	thousand	opposite	crisp	west	contest	Thursday
season	president	deserve	ask	cost	minister	wisdom
poison	pleasant	result	basket	worst	yesterday	cosmetics
chosen	unpleasant	museum	rescue	least	almost	

2 Read the sentences. Above each underlined _s_ or _ss_, write _s_ or _z_ to show which sound it has, as shown in number 1.

1. The president deserves our support.

2. Deposit that money in the bank. It will earn interest.

3. She has music lessons on Thursdays and Saturdays.

4. I won a thousand dollars in that contest. It was easy!

5. She had a pleasant visit with her cousin.

6. In the hospital my husband had his wisdom teeth removed.

7. That rat poison costs at least four dollars a box.

8. The art museum is on the east side of town.

9. I put the crisp fried chicken in the basket.

10. Last fall our team had the worst season ever.

11. Yesterday the minister was preaching against stealing.

12. The two cousins sat on opposite sides of the room.

13. Are you interested in the results of the contest?

14. Her husband was chosen as the next president.

15. I asked her how much the cosmetics cost.

16. On Tuesday he was busy cleaning out his desk.

17. The hot weather in the west was very unpleasant.

18. It wasn't easy to find things in that messy closet.

19. My baby was almost poisoned when he ate aspirin.

The rescue team took him to the hospital.

Practice 17-D: Two Sounds for Final *se*: /s/ and /z/

1

C + se

When a word ends with a consonant and *se*,

se = /s/

fal<u>se</u>	hor<u>se</u>
el<u>se</u>	nur<u>se</u>
rin<u>se</u>	pur<u>se</u>
sen<u>se</u>	wor<u>se</u>
licen<u>se</u>	cour<u>se</u>
expen<u>se</u>	

V + se

When a word ends with a vowel and *se*,

se = /s/

ca<u>se</u>	lea<u>se</u>
cha<u>se</u>	grea<u>se</u>
era<u>se</u>	increa<u>se</u>
do<u>se</u>	loo<u>se</u>
mou<u>se</u>	purpo<u>se</u>
hou<u>se</u>	

se = /z/

the<u>se</u>	choo<u>se</u>
lo<u>se</u>	chee<u>se</u>
who<u>se</u>	becau<u>se</u>
rai<u>se</u>	disea<u>se</u>
noi<u>se</u>	surpri<u>se</u>
plea<u>se</u>	adverti<u>se</u>

2

Read the sentences. Above each underlined *s*, *ss*, or *se*, write *s* or *z* to show which sound it has, as shown in number 1.

Review word: answer

1. A large do<u>s</u>e of that drug will cure the di<u>s</u>ea<u>s</u>e.

2. If they rai<u>se</u> the rent, we won't sign the lea<u>se</u>.

3. Who<u>se</u> pur<u>se</u> is this? Did Sue lo<u>se</u> hers?

4. We served chee<u>se</u> sandwiches at the <u>s</u>urpri<u>se</u> party.

5. The nur<u>se</u> told us that the sick man felt wor<u>se</u>.

6. This belt is too loo<u>se</u>. I refu<u>se</u> to wear it.

7. I have sen<u>se</u>. I save money in ca<u>se</u> my expen<u>se</u>s increa<u>se</u>.

8. That dre<u>ss</u> looks awful. Choo<u>se</u> something el<u>se</u> to wear.

9. Of cour<u>se</u>, you must never spread tho<u>se</u> fal<u>se</u> stories.

10. He's worried becau<u>se</u> he lost his driver's licen<u>se</u>.

11. Plea<u>se</u> grea<u>se</u> the<u>se</u> pans with butter.

12. Did it surpri<u>se</u> you that no one el<u>se</u> knew the answer?

13. We bought a new hou<u>se</u> becau<u>se</u> we needed more space.

14. Rai<u>se</u> your voice. I can't hear you above this noi<u>se</u>.

15. The cat was too lazy to cha<u>se</u> the mou<u>se</u>.

16. The purpo<u>se</u> of adverti<u>s</u>ing is to increa<u>se</u> bu<u>s</u>ine<u>ss</u>.

17. I did wor<u>se</u> than I thought in that math cour<u>se</u>.

18. That shirt has grea<u>se</u> stains. Rin<u>se</u> it in hot water.

19. That hor<u>se</u> often lo<u>se</u>s in the races.

20. Did he era<u>se</u> the wrong answers on that true-fal<u>se</u> test?

Practice 17-E: Two Other Sounds for *s:* **/zh/ and /sh/**

1 s = /zh/   s = /sh/   ss = /sh/

us̲ual	leis̲ure	s̲ugar	is̲sue
us̲ually	meas̲ure	s̲ure	tis̲sue
unus̲ual	pleas̲ure	s̲urely	pres̲sure
vis̲ual	treas̲ure	ins̲ure	as̲sure
cas̲ual	treas̲ury	ins̲urance	as̲surance
	treas̲urer		reas̲sure

2 Write the word you hear.

1. _____   8. _____   15. _____

2. _____   9. _____   16. _____

3. _____   10. _____   17. _____

4. _____   11. _____   18. _____

5. _____   12. _____   19. _____

6. _____   13. _____   20. _____

7. _____   14. _____   21. _____

3 Read the sentences.   **New word:** amount

1. What do you do for pleasure in your leisure time?

2. We usually dress in casual clothes for school.

3. The doctor reassured me that my blood pressure was fine.

4. Be sure to pick up a box of tissues at the store.

5. The treasurer usually handles large amounts of money.

6. The school children surely enjoy visual aids.

7. The insurance company assured us they would pay.

8. Measure one cup of sugar for the cookies.

9. His disease is unusual, but I'm sure it can be cured.

10. Treasures in the museum are insured for a large amount.

11. He assured me he had studied the tax issue.

12. As usual, he is mixing business with pleasure.

13. Car insurance rates have surely gone up.

14. What amount did the bank send to the treasury?

15. I'm under pressure to get this month's issue out on time.

16. What assurance do we have that he will keep his word?

17. I treasure the unusual ring she gave me.

18. Her tape measure was not in the usual place.

Practice 17-F: *ch* = /ch/ in Most Words

1

ch		SV + tch			V + C + ch	V + V + ch
At the beginning of a word		After a short vowel sound, /ch/ is usually spelled *tch* →		except in words like these: ↓	After a vowel and a consonant	After a long vowel or other vowel sound
children	choose	catch	crutch	rich	inch	each
check	chance	match	sketch	which	lunch	teach
Charles	charge	scratch	watch	sandwich	branch	reach
chapter	chart	itch	kitchen	much	march	speech
chocolate	choice	switch	Mitchell	such	church	coach
chip	child	stitch	pitcher	touch	porch	couch

2 Read the sentences.   **Review words:** I'd, I've

1. I've got a pitcher of punch in the kitchen.

2. Will you pay by check or charge card?

3. Chapter 6 tells how to choose a used car.

4. I said I'd serve lunch on the porch.

5. Measure the box. Is it ten inches long?

6. The nurse checked each child's chart.

7. We marched out of church after his speech.

8. The art teacher looked at each sketch.

9. He reached up to touch the tree branch.

10. I hoped I'd get a chance to see Charles.

11. Mrs. Mitchell put a sandwich in the lunch basket.

12. I've made a chocolate cake for the church bake sale.

13. That rash will itch much more if you scratch it.

14. Charles Mitchell sat on the couch, watching TV.

15. The rich lady buys shoes which match her hats.

16. The coach made the choice to switch players.

17. Measure the flour to make chocolate chip cookies.

18. He's such a good coach! I've learned so much!

19. I'd like to catch the thief who stole my watch.

20. When I had stitches in my foot, I walked with crutches.

3 Write the word you hear.

1. _____

2. _____

3. _____

4. _____

5. _____

6. _____

7. _____

8. _____

9. _____

10. _____

Practice 17-G: *ch* = /k/ in Some Words

1 ch = /k/ in some words.

Chris	character	Michael	ache
Christ		mechanic	headache
Christmas		orchestra	stomach
chorus		orchid	
choir	school	anchor	
chemistry	schedule		
chemical	scheme		

2 Write the word you hear.

1. _____   8. _____

2. _____   9. _____

3. _____   10. _____

4. _____   11. _____

5. _____   12. _____

6. _____   13. _____

7. _____   14. _____

3 Read the sentences. Above each underlined *ch*, write *ch* or *k* to show which sound it has, as shown in number 1.

Review words: here's, what's

1.   k   ch   k   k
  Michael Mitchell plays in the school orchestra.

2. Our chemistry teacher is checking the chemicals in the lab.

3. The church tells us that Christmas is Christ's birthday.

4. Here's some aspirin for your headache.

5. Chris told Chuck he wants to become a mechanic.

6. Charles and Michael got a chance to sing in the chorus.

7. Chris was one of the characters in the Christmas play.

8. My back aches. Can I schedule a visit with the doctor?

9. Drop the anchor to keep the boat from moving.

10. "What's wrong with my car?" Chris asked the mechanic.

11. Michael got a bad stomach ache after he ate the chicken.

12. The orchestra played a march, and then the choir sang.

13. Here's my high school class schedule.

    I have chemistry at ten, choir at one, and speech at two.

14. Charles Mitchell will teach the chorus this year.

15. The children have a scheme to skip school and watch TV.

16. The mechanic said he had an upset stomach.

17. He gave my sister Chris an orchid for Christmas.

Practice 17-H: *ch* = /sh/ in a Few Words

1 ch = /sh/ in a few words.

Chicago   chauffeur   machine

Charlotte   chaperone   brochure

Charlene   chandelier   parachute

Cheryl   champagne

chef

Chevy

Chevrolet   mustache

2 Write the word you hear.

1. _____ 8. _____

2. _____ 9. _____

3. _____ 10. _____

4. _____ 11. _____

5. _____ 12. _____

6. _____

7. _____

3 Read the sentences. Above each underlined *ch*, write *ch*, *k*, or *sh* to show which sound it has, as shown in number 1.

Review word: doesn't

  ch   ch sh   k
1. Charles gave a speech at a Chicago school.

2. The chef chose some champagne to serve with the cheese.

3. This brochure gives the schedule for the city orchestra.

4. The children put too much soap in the washing machine.

5. The mechanic fixed Charlene's old Chevy.

6. He jumped from the plane and opened his parachute.

7. Cheryl married Michael Mitchell on Christmas Day.

8. Charlotte never had a chance to take chemistry.

9. Chris doesn't plan to shave off his mustache.

10. Cheryl made chicken sandwiches for lunch.

11. He has such a beautiful chandelier in the living room!

12. Chris doesn't want to be a chaperone at the school dance.

13. Charles watched the chef make a chocolate cake.

14. That chemical plant in Chicago was shut down March 1.

15. Charlene and Charlotte sing in the church choir.

16. Don't touch the switch on that machine.

17. Too much rich food can give you a stomach ache.

18. The chauffeur drove me to church in the Chevrolet.

Practice 18-A: *c* = /k/

1 When *c* comes before a consonant,

c = /k/

classroom	cry	clock	act	October
club	crowd	truck	exact	doctor
clothes	cruel	black	direct	factory
closet	scream	lucky	protect	picture
include	describe	ticket	elect	tractor
uncle	prescription	hockey	expect	election

When *c* comes at the end of a word,

c = /k/

music	basic
public	panic
traffic	plastic
clinic	picnic
attic	romantic
fabric	electric

2 Read the sentences.   **Review words:** Monday, they'll

1. A doctor at the clinic gave me this prescription.

2. My uncle was lucky to get tickets to this hockey game.

3. We expect they'll win in the election this October.

4. Carry the old clothes in this closet up to the attic.

5. When the man screamed, the crowd started to panic.

6. My electric clock tells the exact time.

7. The cop acted quickly to direct traffic.

8. His classes include speech, music, and basic math.

9. Put the plastic spoons in the picnic basket.

10. We ordered a tractor from the factory last October.

11. Our public school classrooms are too crowded.

12. A large black truck was blocking traffic.

13. That factory makes clothes from fine fabrics.

14. She tried to protect her son from his cruel father.

15. On Monday we will elect the club president.

16. He tried to describe the beautiful picture.

17. That romantic love story made me cry.

18. They'll visit the public health clinic on Monday.

19. My uncle fixed our electric fan.

20. She acted in the play, and I directed it.

Practice 18-B: Two Sounds for *c*: /k/ and /s/

1

c = /k/

before *a*, *o*, or *u*.

call	copy	cut
captain	company	cure
cabin	score	Cuba
scarf	welcome	discuss
became	record	excuse
America	second	secure

c = /s/

before *e*, *i*, or *y*.

center	sentence	December	circus	cycle
cereal	cancer	grocery	medicine	bicycle
certain	recent	city	decide	icy
face	service	citizen	excite	fancy
force	justice	cigarette	pencil	mercy
divorce	practice	circle	recipe	Nancy

2

Read the sentences. Above each underlined *c*, write *k* or *s* to show which sound it has, as shown in number 1.

Review words: police, notice, once, receive

1. Give me a pen**s**cil. I want to **k**copy this re**s**cipe.

2. The team captain decided to keep a record of our scores.

3. When my bicycle was stolen, I called the city police.

4. Is it certain that cigarettes cause cancer?

5. She received a warm welcome from the company president.

6. He gets out of the service the second week of December.

7. I couldn't force Nancy to discuss her recent divorce.

8. He wanted justice, and he had no mercy for the thief.

9. Doctors want to find medicines that will cure cancer.

10. I decided to take my cycle to a mechanic for service.

11. Did you notice the cut on Nancy's face?

12. The police car circled the shopping center once.

13. He came to America from Cuba. He became a U.S. citizen.

14. Nancy got excited once she noticed the circus clowns.

15. We drove along the icy road until we came to the cabin.

16. He bought cereal and fancy cookies at the grocery store.

17. "Copy the sentences on the board," the teacher directed.

18. Her children feel secure at the day care center.

19. Excuse me. I'm sorry I'm late for practice.

20. She put on a fancy dress and a bright red scarf.

Practice 18-C: Two Sounds for *cc***: /k/ and /ks/**

1   cc = /k/
before *a*, *o*, or *u*.

occasion	accomplish	occupation
moccasin	accompany	occupy
according	raccoon	occur
accordian	broccoli	accuse
account	tobacco	accurate

cc = /ks/
before *e* or *i*.

accept	accident
accent	
succeed	
success	
access	

---

2   Read the sentences. Above each underlined *cc*, write *k* or *ks* to show which sound it has, as shown in number 1.

Review words: Friday, possible

          ks   k

1. Is it possible to succeed in that occupation?

2. Did the accident occur on Friday?

3. Please accompany me on your accordian.

4. According to him, this story is accurate.

5. Christmas is always a happy occasion for us.

6. We saw a raccoon in the woods.

7. The Indian wore leather moccasins.

8. I've got access to the bank account records.

9. He put some tobacco in his pipe.

10. Please accept my best wishes for your success.

11. How long did they occupy that house?

12. Cook the broccoli in boiling water.

13. She speaks with an accent.

14. Did you accuse him of stealing?

15. It's not possible to accomplish what we want.

16. She accepted our gift without thanks.

17. Can he accompany me to the doctor's on Friday?

18. The farmer had no success in growing tobacco.

19. I accused her of causing the accident.

20. I had no occasion to use my charge account.

21. His accent makes him hard to understand.

22. This street gives you access to the main road.

3   Write the word you hear.

1. _____

2. _____

3. _____

4. _____

5. _____

6. _____

7. _____

8. _____

9. _____

10. _____

11. _____

Practice 18-D: $g = /g/$

1

When *g* comes before a consonant,

g = /g/

glad	grade	grandfather
glass	Grace	grandchildren
Gladys	green	angry
glue	grow	hungry
English	group	agree
bugle	graduate	degree

When *g* comes at the end of a word,

g = /g/

big	flag
dig	drag
hug	drug
rug	plug
leg	dog
beg	fog

When a word has *gg*,

gg = /g/

egg
foggy
bigger
biggest
stagger
wiggle

2 Read the sentences. **Review word:** front

1. Her grandfather doesn't speak English.

2. I'll graduate with a degree in music.

3. Our dog begs for food when he is hungry.

4. Drag that green rug into the front room.

5. It's so foggy out, I can't see.

6. Blow the bugle when they raise the flag.

7. Grace has six grandchildren.

8. We couldn't agree on the biggest issue.

9. The little kids wiggle in their seats.

10. I get angry when dogs dig up my yard.

11. I'm glad I'm teaching the second grade.

12. He tripped on the rug and hurt his leg.

13. Grandfather gave Gladys a big hug.

14. He bought some glue at the drug store.

15. I ate an egg and drank a glass of milk.

16. Big green bushes grow in my front yard.

17. The group grew bigger and more angry.

18. I'll be glad when this fog lifts.

19. Gladys plugged in the lamp.

20. He staggered out, high on drugs.

3 Double the last *g* and add the ending to the root word, as shown in number 1. Read the new word.

1. fog + g + y   *foggy*

2. bag + g + y   _____

3. smog + g + y   _____

4. big + g + er   _____

5. dig + g + er   _____

6. mug + g + er   _____

7. brag + g + ing   _____

8. hug + g + ing   _____

9. beg + g + ed   _____

Practice 18-E: Two Sounds for g: /g/ and /j/

1 **g = /g/**

before *a*, *o*, or *u*.

gave	good	gun
gallon	gone	guy
garden	Gordon	gulf
again	government	begun
against	ago	argue
began	forgot	August

g = /j/

before *e*, *i*, or *y*.

Gene	general	Roger	engine	gym
George	budget	Ginger	region	gypsy
gentle	urgent	giant	rigid	energy
gentleman	refugee	giraffe	imagine	geology
generous	manager	magic	religion	stingy
germ	agency	tragic	register	apology

2 But note these few *ge* and *gi* words in which g = /g/.

get	girl
geese	gift
gear	give
forget	given
together	forgive
target	begin
eager	giggle
anger	girdle
hunger	gizzard
finger	

3 Read the sentences. Above each underlined *g*, write *g* or *j* to show which sound it has, as shown in number 1.   **Review word:** let's

    g   j   j
1. I argued with the manager of the agency.
2. Gene is eager to plan the budget.
3. Did he forget to get a gallon of milk?
4. He is generous with gifts, not stingy.
5. Gordon is against the use of guns.
6. Ginger became manager a year ago.
7. Accept my apology and forgive me.
8. Roger began to speak in a gentle voice.
9. George got a good picture of the gypsy.
10. Gordon helped a girl register to vote.

11. Let's get together with Gene at the gym.
12. Start the engine again and put it in gear.
13. Her religion teaches that God forgives.
14. Roger called you, but it wasn't urgent.
15. The general never forgot the tragic war.
16. George gave me some seeds for my garden.
17. The food I was given was gone by August.
18. The government will help the refugees.
19. Imagine a magic land full of giants!
20. Let's begin to find new energy sources.

Practice 18-F: Final *ge* and *dge* = /j/

1

SV + dge	V + C + ge		LV + ge	V + ge		
After a short vowel, /j/ is spelled *dge*.	After a vowel and a consonant, /j/ is spelled *ge*.		After a long vowel, /j/ is spelled *ge*.	After a vowel in an unstressed syllable, /j/ is spelled *ge*.		
edge	large	arrange	age	bandage	luggage	average
judge	Marge	lounge	cage	courage	baggage	beverage
pledge	urge	orange	page	damage	village	language
bridge	range		wage	garbage	cabbage	marriage
lodge	change		stage	manage	cottage	sausage
	strange		huge	package	college	shortage

2 Read the sentences.   **Review words:** young, different, danger, passenger, emergency, Dodgers

1. We had sausage, cabbage, and a hot beverage for dinner.

2. Get some bandages from the emergency first aid kit.

3. Gordon had great courage to face that danger.

4. Put that large orange rug in the lounge.

5. The passenger carried luggage and packages on the plane.

6. I urged the young woman not to rush into marriage.

7. The Dodgers drew a huge crowd of people of all ages.

8. Marge manages the stage crews for all the college plays.

9. The judge can arrange to have Gene let out of jail.

10. I'll change to a different college to study languages.

11. The young children rose and said the pledge to the flag.

12. Passengers claim their baggage and change trains here.

13. This cottage cheese is spoiled. Toss it in the garbage.

14. The judge granted George $500 in damages.

15. In this village, they speak many different languages.

16. My job cleaning the lodge pays average wages.

17. The bridge is in danger of giving way.

18. We saw strange birds in different cages at the zoo.

19. Marge loves cooking with her new electric range.

20. Someone wrote notes on the edge of page 67.

Practice 18-G: *gu* = /g/ before a Vowel

1 **gu = /g/** before a vowel.

The *u* is silent.		The *ue* is silent.	
guard	guilt	league	synogogue
guardian	guilty	morgue	catalogue (catalog)
guess	guitar	vague	
guest	guarantee	plague	
guide	disguise	fatigue	

2 Write the word you hear.

1. _____   6. _____   11. _____

2. _____   7. _____   12. _____

3. _____   8. _____   13. _____

4. _____   9. _____   14. _____

5. _____   10. _____   15. _____

3 Read the sentences.   **New word:** taken   **Review words:** themselves, question, tomorrow

1. Tell the guests to help themselves to the food.

2. Our Little League team plays tomorrow.

3. A guard will guide the guests through the jail.

4. We knew he was guilty, but we couldn't prove his guilt.

5. People who died in the plague were taken to the morgue.

6. I'll wear that disguise to the costume party tomorrow.

7. Her guitar was taken. Can you guess who took it?

8. I didn't understand his vague answer to my question.

9. The mechanics guarantee their work.

10. He ordered a guitar from a mail order catalogue.

11. A guardian has taken care of the children for years.

12. Marge felt fatigue because of a lack of sleep.

13. In this disguise, no one will guess who I am.

14. This city has many churches and synagogues.

15. The guard felt guilty when the thief got away.

16. Tomorrow the players in the football league will meet.

17. We have a one-year guarantee on our new car.

18. He tried to guess the answers to the test questions.

19. This map is your guide to the city.

20. Write down the name of your parent or guardian.

Practice 18-H: Review of *s*, *ch*, *c*, and *g*

1 Look at the picture and say the word. Then write the word.

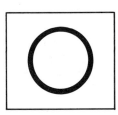

_____   _____   _____

_____   _____   _____

2 Read the sentences. Above each underlined letter or letters, write *s*, *z*, *ch*, *k*, *ks*, *sh*, *g*, or *j* to show which sound it has, as shown in number 1.

1. In Au͟g͟ust C͟h͟arles be͟c͟ame an Ameri͟c͟an ͟ci͟tizen.
   (g) (ch)   (k)   (k) (s)

2. Mi͟chael hope͟s to ͟go to a busine͟ss ͟college in Chi͟ca͟go.

3. Do͟ctors at the clini͟c are ͟certain ͟Gordon ha͟s ͟can͟cer.

4. ͟Gene, our Little Lea͟gue ͟coa͟ch, is a Dod͟gers fan.

5. ͟Ginger i͟s baking ͟chocolate ͟chip ͟cookie͟s for ͟Christma͟s.

6. We had ͟chicken ͟sandwi͟ches and ͟cotta͟ge ͟chee͟se for lun͟ch.

7. ͟Chris i͟s eager to ͟guide u͟s through the a͟gen͟cy.

8. When did that fa͟ctory a͟ccident o͟ccur? I'm not ͟sure.

9. ͟Cheryl asked the do͟ctor to ͟check her blood pre͟ssure.

3 Say the first word in the box. Then put a circle around any word on that line that rhymes with that word.

chase	case	raise	vase	cheese	erase	place	chose
cage	badge	wage	stage	cape	page	bag	age
face	Grace	place	page	case	space	fake	vase
rise	rose	wise	nice	size	rice	prize	raise
such	much	rush	chef	touch	catch	suck	crutch

4 Make at least 11 words with these beginnings and endings:

ba	ge
ri	ce
pa	dge
do	tch
ca	se

_____   _____   _____

_____   _____   _____

_____   _____   _____

_____   _____   _____

_____   _____   _____

Practice 18-I: The Ending -en

1 The ending -en is added to some verbs to make the form of the verb that is used after *has*, *have*, or *had*.

Add -en to the verbs below, as shown in these examples:

vvc
eat + **en** ➡ **eaten**

cvc
got + **t** + **en** ➡ **gotten**

give + **n** ➡ **given**

broke   1. Michael has _**broken**_ his leg.

hid   2. We have _____ the money.

take   3. Larry had _____ the bus home.

prove   4. She had _____ his guilt.

beat   5. They have _____ our team.

forgive   6. Have they _____ each other?

bit   7. A dog had _____ Gladys.

stole   8. Who had _____ the cash?

fall   9. George had _____ on the ice.

chose   10. Gordon has _____ a book to read.

forgot   11. Jerry had _____ his keys.

spoke   12. Has Cheryl _____ to Roger?

In these words, the vowel sound changes when -en is added.

rise   13. The sun has _____.

drive   14. Gene had not _____ the van.

2 The ending -en is also added to many adjectives to change them into verbs. Then -en means "to make" or "to become."

Add -en to the words below, as shown in the first sentence.

wide   1. The road crew will _**widen**_ this street.

sharp   2. Please _____ this knife for me.

moist   3. We will _____ the soil around the plant.

fat   4. Farmers _____ up the pigs for market.

thick   5. Add some flour to _____ the sauce.

sweet   6. I _____ my coffee with sugar.

tight, loose   7. Should I _____ this screw

or _____ it?

hard, soft   8. Did the butter _____?

Leave it out to _____ it.

less, deep   9. This shot will _____ the pain

and _____ your sleep.

worse, short   10. Smoking can _____ a person's health

and _____ a person's life.

dark, light   11. This dye will _____ my hair color,

not _____ it.

threat   12. Did that man _____ you with a gun?

fright   13. Horror movies _____ me.

red, ripe   14. Apples _____ as they _____.

Practice 19-A: *wr* = /r/ and *wh* = /h/

1 wr = /r/

wh = /h/
in a few words.

wrap	wring	wrong	who
wreck	wrinkle		whom
wren	wrist		whose
wrench	write		whole
wrestle	writer		whoever
wrestler	written		
wreath	wrote		

2 Write the word you hear.

1. _____   8. _____   15. _____

2. _____   9. _____   16. _____

3. _____   10. _____   17. _____

4. _____   11. _____   18. _____

5. _____   12. _____   19. _____

6. _____   13. _____   20. _____

7. _____   14. _____

3 Read the sentences.

1. Who will fight that wrestler?

2. I had written down the wrong address.

3. That car is a wreck! Whose is it?

4. She wrote down the whole story.

5. Give the wrench to whoever needs it.

6. Hang the Christmas wreath in the window.

7. Press the dress to get the wrinkles out.

8. The wren is a small bird that sings.

9. She wrapped a bandage around his wrist.

10. The writer worked the whole day.

11. Wring out your wet shirt.

12. I saw the cops wrestle with the thief.

13. The man to whom I spoke is a writer.

14. Who will wrap up these gifts?

15. My wrist is hurt. I cannot write.

16. That fire wrecked the whole house.

17. That wrench is the wrong size.

18. Whom did you write to last week?

4 Homonyms: whole and hole

He ate the whole apple.

I gave her a whole set of dishes.

Put the button through the hole.

They dug a large hole.

They filled up the _____ in the road.

Our _____ team was there.

I read the _____ book yesterday.

My sock has a _____ in it.

Gene slept the _____ night.

Practice 19-B: *kn* = /n/ and *gn* = /n/

1 kn = /n/   gn = /n/

<u>kn</u>it	<u>kn</u>ow	<u>kn</u>owledge	si<u>gn</u>	<u>gn</u>aw
<u>kn</u>ob	<u>kn</u>own	<u>kn</u>apsack	assi<u>gn</u>	
<u>kn</u>ot	<u>kn</u>ew	un<u>kn</u>own	desi<u>gn</u>	
<u>kn</u>ock	<u>kn</u>ife		resi<u>gn</u>	
<u>kn</u>ee	<u>kn</u>ives		forei<u>gn</u>	
<u>kn</u>eel	<u>kn</u>ight		campai<u>gn</u>	
<u>kn</u>ead	<u>kn</u>uckle		rei<u>gn</u>	

2 Write the word you hear.

1. _____   8. _____   15. _____

2. _____   9. _____   16. _____

3. _____   10. _____   17. _____

4. _____   11. _____   18. _____

5. _____   12. _____   19. _____

6. _____   13. _____   20. _____

7. _____   14. _____   21. _____

3 Read the sentences.

1. No one answered when he knocked.

   So he turned the knob and went in.

2. We have known many foreign students.

3. Do you know how to tie a square knot?

4. That knit sweater has a lovely design.

5. She put the knife back in her knapsack.

6. Support our campaign by signing a check.

7. I hurt my knuckles knocking on the door.

8. The king who reigned made him a knight.

9. He knew how to knead the bread dough.

10. Do you know where to put the knives?

11. He was afraid of the unknown.

12. She kneels down to paint the sign.

13. I was assigned to work on the campaign.

14. The player knew he had hurt his knee.

15. I had no knowledge of who would resign.

16. Gene helps design foreign cars.

17. The dog was gnawing on the bone.

4 Homonyms: <u>knot</u> and <u>not</u>

Can you untie this <u>knot</u>?

He <u>knots</u> his shoelaces.

She's <u>not</u> going to the party.

The rope is tied in a square _____ .

Ginger is _____ feeling well.

_____ the thread for me.

That book was _____ interesting.

I do _____ have any change.

Practice 19-C: *mb* = /m/, *bt* = /t/, and *mn* = /m/

1 mb = /m/   bt = /t/   mn = /m/

lamb	plumber	debt	damn
limb	comb	doubt	hymn
bomb	climb	doubtful	autumn
dumb	womb		column
numb	tomb		condemn
thumb			solemn
crumb			

2 Write the word you hear.

1. _____   8. _____   15. _____

2. _____   9. _____   16. _____

3. _____   10. _____   17. _____

4. _____   11. _____   18. _____

5. _____   12. _____   19. _____

6. _____   13. _____   20. _____

7. _____   14. _____   21. _____

3 Read the sentences.   **Review words:** animal, body

1. The plumber hurt his thumb.

2. She climbed up on the tree limb.

3. We were solemn as we sang the hymn.

4. It is doubtful that he paid his debts.

5. Animals are dumb. They can't speak.

6. The dead body was put into the tomb.

7. Lambs are the animals that give us wool.

8. Please wipe the crumbs off the table.

9. My body was numb with cold.

10. I doubt such a dumb plan will work.

11. He condemned the book. He damned it.

12. The baby is safe in its mother's womb.

13. Did you read that column on the front page?

14. After the bomb went off, we felt numb.

15. This autumn we went mountain climbing.

16. Ginger combs her long blond hair.

17. They condemn the use of bombs and guns.

18. We doubt if a plumber can fix the leak.

4 Homonyms: knead and need

She's kneading the bread dough.

Does he need any money?

They are in need of clothes.

_____ the flour into the dough.

She was a friend in _____.

Please _____ that bread dough.

Plants _____ water.

The children's _____s are great.

Practice 19-D: Silent _h_, _rh_ = /r/, and _gh_ = /g/

1 At the beginning of a few words, the _h_ is silent

ĥ   rh = /r/   gh = /g/

hour   honor   rhyme   ghost

heir   honorable   rhythm   ghetto

heiress   rhubarb   spaghetti

herb   rhinoceros

honest   rheumatism

honesty

dishonest

2 Write the word you hear.

1. _____   8. _____   15. _____

2. _____   9. _____

3. _____   10. _____

4. _____   11. _____

5. _____   12. _____

6. _____   13. _____

7. _____   14. _____

3 Read the sentences.   **Review words:** adult, older, able, important, finish

1. Season the spaghetti sauce with herbs.

2. That song has both rhyme and rhythm.

3. This book is honest about ghetto life.

4. The will named Marge as the heiress.

5. This rhubarb pie has to bake an hour.

6. Some older adults get rheumatism.

7. Honesty is important to honorable men.

8. Our zoo was able to get a rhinoceros.

9. Has Gene finished picking the rhubarb?

10. George was the man's only adult heir.

11. Are you able to finish your spaghetti?

12. Was the president honest or dishonest?

13. She was honored for her important work.

14. Roger grew up in a Chicago ghetto.

15. I told ghost stories to the older kids.

16. Prince Charles is heir to the throne.

17. A party to honor him starts in an hour.

18. We danced to the rhythm of the music.

4 **Homonyms:** heir and air

He is heir to a fortune.

Please air out this room.

We need air to breathe.

We smelled smoke in the _____.

That _____ will soon be rich.

I have to _____ out the closet.

He chose his son as _____.

Let in some fresh _____.

Practice 19-E: Silent _t_

1 In many words, _t_ is silent.

t̸   et = /ā/

often	castle	bustle	ballet
soften	wrestle	rustle	buffet
	wrestler	rustler	fillet
fasten	whistle		bouquet
listen	thistle		croquet
glisten	bristle		crochet
Christmas	hustle		

2 Write the word you hear.

1. _____   8. _____   15. _____

2. _____   9. _____   16. _____

3. _____   10. _____   17. _____

4. _____   11. _____   18. _____

5. _____   12. _____   19. _____

6. _____   13. _____   20. _____

7. _____   14. _____   21. _____

3 Read the sentences.

1. Listen for the sound of the whistle.

2. We ate fish fillets at the buffet.

3. Christmas shoppers hustle and bustle.

4. The leaves rustled in the wind.

5. Soften the butter and add the sugar.

6. The ballet dancer got a bouquet of roses.

7. Her jewels glisten in the light.

8. The wrestlers hustled to the gym.

9. Use this pin to fasten the dress.

10. She often wins when we play croquet.

11. This brush has hard stiff bristles.

12. The rustlers stole many horses.

13. We listened to the Christmas songs.

14. Kings often live in castles.

15. The cop wrestled with the robber.

16. The thistle plant has pretty flowers.

17. Cheryl loves to knit and crochet.

18. Gene likes to whistle at pretty girls.

4 **Homonyms:** reign and rein

The ruler reigned ten years.

His reign was a powerful one.

Pull the reins to stop the horse.

He reined his horse gently.

Hold on to the _____s.

How long did the queen _____?

_____ in your horse!

The king's _____ lasted ten years.

The queen _____s over the people.

1   **Silent *l***   **ps = /s/**

ta<u>l</u>k	ca<u>l</u>f	cou<u>l</u>d
wa<u>l</u>k	ha<u>l</u>f	wou<u>l</u>d
cha<u>l</u>k	ca<u>l</u>ves	shou<u>l</u>d
sta<u>l</u>k	ha<u>l</u>ves	
sidewa<u>l</u>k	ca<u>l</u>m	
fo<u>l</u>k	pa<u>l</u>m	
yo<u>l</u>k	sa<u>l</u>mon	

<u>p</u>salm

<u>p</u>sychology

<u>p</u>sychologist

<u>p</u>sychiatrist

pt = /t/

recei<u>pt</u>

2 Write the word you hear.

1. _____	8. _____	15. _____
2. _____	9. _____	16. _____
3. _____	10. _____	17. _____
4. _____	11. _____	18. _____
5. _____	12. _____	19. _____
6. _____	13. _____	20. _____
7. _____	14. _____	21. _____

3 Read the sentences.   **Review word:** problem

1. Could you give me a receipt?

2. Two halves make one whole.

3. She should talk to a psychiatrist.

4. Walk on the sidewalk, not on the road.

5. The minister read one of the psalms.

6. No one would talk about the problem.

7. The teacher used half a box of chalk.

8. The calf had a problem walking.

9. My folks have palm trees in their yard.

10. He told the psychologist the problem.

    The psychologist helped him calm down.

11. The ring is in the palm of her hand.

12. Those folks could not catch any salmon.

13. Corn grows on tall stalks.

14. She would like to study psychology.

15. The farmer would not sell his calves.

16. Beat the egg yolks with a fork.

17. You should stay calm in an emergency.

4 **Homonyms:** Write <u>reign</u>, <u>rein</u>, or <u>rain</u>.

1. Will it _____ tomorrow?

2. The rider dropped the _____s.

3. The royal family had a long _____.

4. The kids won't go out in the _____.

5. Who will _____ over the country?

6. I held tight to the _____s.

7. The king helped people during his _____.

8. The farmers need _____.

9. Stop the horse. _____ him in.

Practice 19-G: Silent *gh*

1 /ī/ /ā/ /aw/ /ō/

/ī/		/ā/	/aw/	/ō/
high	height	weigh	caught	dough
light	flight	weight	taught	though
might	bright	eight	ought	although
night		freight	bought	thorough
right		neighbor	fought	
sight		neighborhood	thought	**/oo/**
fight			brought	through

2 Write the word you hear.

1. _____   8. _____   15. _____
2. _____   9. _____   16. _____
3. _____   10. _____   17. _____
4. _____   11. _____   18. _____
5. _____   12. _____   19. _____
6. _____   13. _____   20. _____
7. _____   14. _____   21. _____

3 Read the sentences.

1. At night we see the bright city lights.

2. I thought he ought to lose weight.

3. Did they ever get through high school?

4. She taught us how to make bread dough.

5. Although I'm sick, I might go to work.

6. He brought his neighbor to the party.

7. The night flight arrives at eight.

8. We thought she did a thorough job.

9. The boys were caught fighting.

10. Our neighbors bought a new car.

11. The sight in her right eye is bad.

12. We fought our way through the crowd.

13. His weight is just right for his height.

14. The box weighs eight pounds. It's light.

15. Trains brought freight to the city.

16. We fight even though we're in love.

17. I'm through reading the book I bought.

18. We might move out of this neighborhood.

4 Homonyms: weight and wait

The dog's weight is 50 pounds.

George lifts weights every day.

Who are you waiting for?

Wait to cross the street.

Did he _____ to take the test?

Has Gordon gained any _____?

You can _____ for me after work.

I have a paper _____ on my desk.

Did the clerk _____ on you yet?

Practice 19-H: *ph* and *gh* = /f/

1 ph = /f/   gh = /f/

photo	telephone	Ralph	rough
phony	elephant	Joseph	tough
Phil	orphan	graph	enough
Phyllis	pamphlet	telegraph	laugh
pharmacy	trophy	photograph	cough
physical	alphabet	photography	
physician	Philadelphia	paragraph	

2 Write the word you hear.

1. _____ 8. _____ 15. _____

2. _____ 9. _____ 16. _____

3. _____ 10. _____ 17. _____

4. _____ 11. _____ 18. _____

5. _____ 12. _____ 19. _____

6. _____ 13. _____ 20. _____

7. _____ 14. _____ 21. _____

3 Read the sentences.

Review words: nephew, phone, information, exam, remember

1. Does Phyllis have enough money for the pay phone?

2. Phil had a cough. A physician gave him a physical exam.

3. Ralph's photography won first prize. He got a trophy.

4. An elephant is an unusual animal. It has a long trunk.

5. She started to laugh when she looked at Phil's photos.

6. The news was sent by telephone and telegraph.

7. He remembered enough information to pass the tough exam.

8. My nephew is in first grade. He's learning his alphabet.

9. Joseph showed the cop a phony driver's license.

10. This pamphlet tells how to take good photographs.

11. The meat was too tough for Phyllis to eat.

12. Did the physician remember to phone the pharmacy?

13. The graph shows an unusual drop in sales over the year.

14. The road we took to Philadelphia was rough, not smooth.

15. This paragraph doesn't give enough information.

16. Joseph's nephew owns a pharmacy in Philadelphia.

17. Phil took photographs of the elephants at the zoo.

18. Ralph was an orphan who grew up in a rough neighborhood.

Practice 19-I: Review of Other Consonant Spellings

1   Look at the picture and say the word. Then write the word.

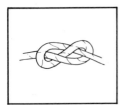  

_____   _____   _____

_____   _____   _____

2   Read the sentences.

1. For hours, I listened to Phil talk about the campaign.

2. That psychologist is well known for the books he wrote.

3. The plumber didn't know who had taken his wrench.

4. Do they have enough salmon and spaghetti at the buffet?

5. The little boy could walk, but he could not climb stairs.

6. Roger bought enough film to take photos of Philadelphia.

7. We thought Ralph was honest, but we could be wrong.

8. I doubt whether the wrestler has gained any weight.

9. Joseph had a cough, so he went to a physician's office.

10. Phyllis spent the whole evening knitting a scarf.

3   Say the first word in the box. Then put a circle around any word on that line that begins with the same sound.

write	wrench	raise	whole	wear	rhyme	whip	rare
phone	rough	pair	photo	fine	face	help	graph
night	next	gnaw	may	knew	fight	never	knot
who	where	hear	high	when	wrap	hour	hand
knock	nice	keep	knee	kick	note	knob	shock

4   Make at least 12 words with these beginnings and endings:

th	umb
d	ough
wh	istle
n	en
wr	ose

_____   _____   _____

_____   _____   _____

_____   _____   _____

_____   _____   _____

_____   _____   _____

1

-tion = /shun/

cau<u>tion</u>

na<u>tion</u>

sec<u>tion</u>

2 Read the words.

nation	auction
station	section
lotion	fiction
motion	friction
portion	fraction
option	function
caution	mention

3 Write the word you hear.

1. _____   8. _____

2. _____   9. _____

3. _____   10. _____

4. _____   11. _____

5. _____   12. _____

6. _____   13. _____

7. _____   14. _____

4 Read the sentences.   **Review words:** present, history, they're

1. Our nation's government functions well.

2. They're leaving for the bus station.

3. Did he mention when the auction is?

4. One section of the test is on fractions.

5. We have many options to choose from.

6. Can you feel the motion of the ship?

7. At present, he runs a service station.

8. They're putting on suntan lotion.

9. Oil reduces friction between car parts.

10. They're studying our nation's history.

11. My birthday present was a fiction book.

12. Give each child a small portion to eat.

13. Use caution in crossing the street.

14. All those present voted on the motion.

15. He was mentioned in the sports section.

16. A caution light functions as a warning.

17. We bought that clock at an auction.

    It sold for a fraction of its value.

5 Mark the stressed syllable, as shown in number 1.

1. auc′ tion   8. por tion

2. frac tion   9. lo tion

3. mo tion   10. fric tion

4. op tion   11. sec tion

5. na tion   12. func tion

6. cau tion   13. sta tion

7. fic tion   14. men tion

Practice 20-B: Final *t* + *-ion* = /shun/

1

— t + ion

act + ion →
action

elect + ion →
election

2 These root words are action words (verbs) that end with *t*. Add *-ion* to each word to make a noun that names the process or result of doing something. Read the new word.

act   *action*   infect   _____

elect   _____   invent   _____

direct   _____   prevent   _____

connect _____   deduct   _____

collect _____   construct   _____

correct _____   attract   _____

protect _____   adopt   _____

3 Read the sentences.   **Review words:** contraction, we'd, insurance

1. The construction crew went into action.

2. Our church took up a collection.

3. Bandages help prevent infection.

4. *We'd* is a contraction of *we would*.

5. Our phone connection is very bad.

6. Insurance protects my coin collection.

7. He was the main attraction at the show.

8. We'd like to see your new invention.

9. They visited the adoption agency.

10. Police work hard at crime prevention.

11. Give me directions to your house.

12. He missed his plane connections.

13. Life insurance gives us protection.

14. We'd support you in the election.

15. George has a bad ear infection.

16. Is there a deduction from my paycheck?

17. Did the insurance company take action?

18. The newspaper printed a correction.

4 Drop *-ion*. Write the root word and then read it.

1. direction   *direct*

2. prevention   _____

3. connection   _____

4. adoption   _____

5. collection   _____

6. deduction   _____

7. invention   _____

8. attraction   _____

9. protection   _____

73

Practice 20-C: Final *te* + -ion = /shun/

1 —t*e* + ion

educate
educat*e* + ion ➡
education

graduate
graduat*e* + ion ➡
graduation

2 These root words are verbs that end with *te*. Drop the *e* and add *-ion* to make a noun that names the process or result of doing something. Read the new word.

educate   *education*
graduate   _____
locate   _____
donate   _____
create   _____
celebrate   _____
operate   _____

decorate   _____
communicate _____
cooperate   _____
illustrate   _____
demonstrate _____
contribute   _____
pollute   _____

3 Read the sentences.

1. We had a celebration after graduation.

2. Her donation was a big contribution.

3. This education book has illustrations.

4. Air pollution is bad in that location.

5. Good communication led to cooperation.

6. I went to a hospital for the operation.

7. Police broke up the demonstration.

8. That school is in a good location.

9. The earth is a beautiful creation.

10. The operation of that machine is easy.

    I'll give you a quick demonstration.

11. There is no communication between them.

12. We will never forget her contributions.

13. Let me give you an illustration.

14. Get some decorations for a celebration.

15. Graduation followed years of education.

16. We need cooperation to fight pollution.

17. She took a class in cake decoration.

4 Drop the ending. Write the root word and then read it.

1. decoration   _____

2. celebration   _____

3. contribution   _____

4. illustration   _____

5. demonstration _____

6. location   _____

7. pollution   _____

8. creation   _____

9. cooperation   _____

Practice 20-D: *-ation*

1

inform
+ ation ➡
information

invite ➡ invit~~e~~
+ ation ➡
invitation

2 Add *-ation* to each verb to make a noun. Read the new word.

inform	*information*
transport	_____
tempt	_____
present	_____
expect	_____
alter	_____
consider	_____

3 These root words are verbs that end with *e*. Drop the *e* and add *-ation* to make a noun. Read the new word.

invite	*invitation*
quote	_____
starve	_____
examine	_____
imagine	_____
combine	_____
reserve	_____

4 Read the sentences.   **Review word:** daily

1. She made some alterations in the suit.

2. He shows no consideration for others.

3. I got information on bus transportation.

4. Please accept our invitation.

5. Your expectations are too high.

6. Many people die of starvation daily.

7. What is the combination to the safe?

8. The doctor made a quick examination.

9. Do you remember that famous quotation?

10. Did you make our plane reservations?

11. The speaker gave a good presentation.

12. They got an invitation to the party.

13. Gene failed the history examination.

14. We use public transportation daily.

15. Ham and eggs are a good combination.

16. Don't give in to temptation.

17. That writer uses his imagination.

18. I got information for a class presentation.

5 Drop *-ation*. Write the root word and then read it.

1. consideration _____

2. reservation _____

3. presentation _____

4. starvation _____

5. combination _____

6. transportation _____

7. imagination _____

8. quotation _____

9. temptation _____

75

Practice 20-E: More *-tion* Words

1 Read these root words and the *-tion* words that come from them.

apply	application
register	registration
occupy	occupation
describe	description
prescribe	prescription
explain	explanation
destroy	destruction

2 Fill in the right *-tion* word.

1. Dr. Hill <u>prescribed</u> some pills. A pharmacy filled the _____.

2. He tried to <u>explain</u> it, but we didn't understand the _____.

3. A fire <u>destroyed</u> the store. The _____ was awful.

4. Sports will <u>occupy</u> his time if his _____ is coaching.

5. I'll <u>apply</u> for that job. Give me an _____.

6. When you <u>register</u> to vote, you fill out a _____ card.

7. <u>Describe</u> the accident. Give me a complete _____.

3 Read these other common *-tion* words.

attention	at ten' tion
vacation	vā cā' tion
emotion	ē mō' tion
affection	af fec' tion
tradition	tra di' tion
condition	con di' tion
reduction	rē duc' tion
production	prō duc' tion
constitution	con sti tū' tion

4 Read the sentences.   **Review word:** voter

1. The application asks for my occupation.

2. Pay attention to my explanation.

3. Have you read the U.S. Constitution?

4. He has great affection for his father.

5. College registration came after vacation.

6. He gave cops a description of the thief.

7. I read a book on weight reduction.

8. Gene resigned without any explanation.

9. She directs motion picture productions.

10. That bomb caused great destruction.

11. That prescription cured his condition.

12. We had a reduction in food production.

13. They paid no attention to tradition.

14. His voice was filled with emotion.

15. Each occupation has a job description.

16. Voter registration ends today.

17. Joseph filled out a job application.

18. Our vacation home is in good condition.

Practice 21-A: *-sion* and *-ssion* = /shun/

1 **-sion** = /shun/

after *n* in some words.

pension   mansion

tension

-ssion = /shun/

mission   session

passion   profession

2 These root words are verbs that end with *ss*. Add *-ion* to make a noun, and read the word.

discuss   *discussion*

impress   _____

depress   _____

express   _____

confess   _____

possess   _____

3 Drop the last *t* in the root word. Add *-ssion* to each verb to make a noun. Read the new word.

admit   _____

permit   _____

transmit   _____

Drop the last *d* in the root word and add *-sion*.

comprehend _____

extend   _____

expand   _____

4 Read the sentences.   **Review word:** unhappy

1. Too much tension caused her depression.

2. We had discussions on the pension plan.

3. She repaired the car's transmission.

4. I stored my possessions in the mansion.

5. Court is now in session.

6. I saw an unhappy expression on her face.

7. Priests at the mission hear confessions.

8. He spoke with passion in the discussion.

9. Expansion of the factory will add space.

10. I'm unhappy in the teaching profession.

11. I get the impression he's under tension.

12. He read the book without comprehension.

13. He gave me permission to drive his car.

14. Guilt and depression led to confession.

15. Two dollars is the price of admission.

16. Who took possession of the mansion?

17. They left earth on a space mission.

18. I got an extension on my bank loan.

5 Write the root word and read it.

1. confession   _____

2. permission   _____

3. extension   _____

4. depression   _____

5. comprehension   _____

6. discussion   _____

7. possession   _____

8. admission   _____

9. expression   _____

1 -sion = /zhun/

in some words.

vision

television

occasion

version

2 Drop the *de* or *se* from the root word.
Add *-sion* to each verb to make a noun.

decide   *decision*

divide   _____

collide   _____

conclude   _____

explode   _____

persuade   _____

confuse   _____

revise   _____

supervise _____

3 Use the *-sion* words in part 2 to fill in these sentences.

1. Two cars had a _____.

2. What a loud _____!

3. This is the second _____ of the book.

4. You'll have to make a _____ soon.

5. Children need close _____.

6. He left the room in great _____.

7. The _____ of the movie was exciting.

8. I can't do these _____ problems.

9. A little _____ will change her mind.

4 Read the sentences.   **Review word:** future

1. In conclusion, I've reached a decision.

2. An explosion followed the car collision.

   There was confusion after the accident.

3. Those division problems were easy.

4. He read the conclusion of the story.

5. She has visions of the future.

6. We watched television on many occasions.

7. He gave his own version of the story.

8. He won me over with his persuasion.

9. Her vision may get worse in the future.

10. Those road signs caused some confusion.

11. People in supervision make decisions.

12. I have collision insurance on my car.

13. This speech needs some revisions.

14. The army division heard the explosion.

15. Television ads are used for persuasion.

5 Write the root word and read it.

1. explosion   _____

2. supervision _____

3. conclusion   _____

4. collision   _____

5. decision   _____

6. confusion   _____

7. persuasion   _____

8. division   _____

Practice 22-A: *ci* = /**sh**/

1

social
-cial
physician
-cian
ancient
-cient
precious
-cious

2 Read the words.

social	physician	conscience
racial	musician	
special	politician	
official	electrician	vicious
artificial		precious
commercial	ancient	conscious
	efficient	delicious
appreciate	sufficient	suspicious

3 Write the word you hear.

1. _____ 9. _____ 17. _____
2. _____ 10. _____ 18. _____
3. _____ 11. _____ 19. _____
4. _____ 12. _____ 20. _____
5. _____ 13. _____
6. _____ 14. _____
7. _____ 15. _____
8. _____ 16. _____

4 Read the sentences.   **New word:** especially   **Review words:** prejudice, self

1. We all appreciated the delicious dinner.

2. The politicians fought a vicious campaign.

3. In social studies class, we talked about racial prejudice.

4. The physician appreciates his nurse. She's efficient.

5. Phyllis is especially self-conscious about her weight.

6. They found precious jewels in the ancient tomb.

7. The musician did not have sufficient time to practice.

8. Government officials have many special duties.

9. I saw a TV commercial for artificial Christmas trees.

10. After spreading vicious lies, he had a guilty conscience.

11. He's suspicious of most people, especially politicians.

12. Efficient people do not waste precious time.

13. The food was delicious at the ice cream social.

14. He is the official president of the electricians' union.

15. A physician checked the woman. She was not conscious.

16. The flowers look real, but they are artificial.

17. The musician played that tune especially for us.

18. When they held a special meeting, we got suspicious.

Practice 22-B: *ti* = /sh/

1

caution → cautious

patient → patience

initial

2 Read the words.

caution ➡ cautious	partial
ambition ➡ ambitious	initial
nutrition ➡ nutritious	potential
superstition ➡ superstitious	essential
patient ➡ patience	negotiate
impatient ➡ impatience	initiate

3 Write the word you hear.

1. _____ 8. _____ 15. _____

2. _____ 9. _____ 16. _____

3. _____ 10. _____ 17. _____

4. _____ 11. _____ 18. _____

5. _____ 12. _____

6. _____ 13. _____

7. _____ 14. _____

4 Read the sentences.   **New word:** early   **Review words:** leader, female, easily

1. We'll initiate new people into the club early next month.

2. That superstitious woman carries a good-luck charm.

3. The nurse brought the patient a nutritious meal.

4. Here is a partial list of guests to invite.

5. Union leaders waited with impatience to negotiate.

6. That drug has potential dangers. Use it with caution.

7. The initials *U.S.* stand for *United States*.

8. Roy is easily fooled. He should be more cautious.

9. The nutrition club had its initial meeting in early May.

10. Good nutrition is essential for a healthy body.

11. Many of our female police officers are potential leaders.

12. Joseph's early ambition was to become a doctor.

13. Ralph has a lot of patience with his children.

14. Slow down when you see the yellow caution light.

15. Be patient. It's too early to initiate action yet.

16. Phil believes in superstitions. He gets scared easily.

17. Ambitious female workers grew impatient for better jobs.

18. It's essential for judges to be fair, not partial.

Practice 22-C: *t* = /ch/ before *u*

1

picture
future
statue
-tu-

2 Read the words.

picture	lecture	statue
future	moisture	actual
nature	fracture	natural
capture	furniture	situation
mixture	signature	congratulate
culture	adventure	century
feature	temperature	fortune
creature	manufacture	fortunate

3 Write the word you hear.

1. _____ 9. _____ 17. _____

2. _____ 10. _____ 18. _____

3. _____ 11. _____ 19. _____

4. _____ 12. _____ 20. _____

5. _____ 13. _____ 21. _____

6. _____ 14. _____ 22. _____

7. _____ 15. _____ 23. _____

8. _____ 16. _____ 24. _____

4 Read the sentences.   **Review word:** speaker

1. That company manufactures fine furniture.

2. She took a picture of an old statue in the park.

3. Let me congratulate you on your good fortune.

4. Those plants need moisture and warm temperatures to grow.

5. Police captured the crook who forged my signature.

6. Our culture has changed a lot in the last century.

7. That store features natural foods.

8. We must be ready for an actual emergency situation.

9. On the nature hike, he fell down and fractured his arm.

10. It is fortunate that we planned ahead for the future.

11. This catalogue tells the actual cost of the furniture.

12. The picture he painted is worth a fortune.

13. This frosting is a mixture of sugar, butter, and milk.

14. That speaker plans to give many lectures in future months.

15. They tried to capture the strange sea creature.

16. Temperatures won't go below freezing. That's fortunate.

17. We saw a double feature—two adventure movies!

18. The speaker was put in an embarrassing situation.

Practice 22-D: The Prefix *re-*

New words: prefix, appear

1 The prefix *re-* is used before many words to give the meaning "again."
Add *re-* to the words below, as shown in the first sentence.

open   1. That store plans to *reopen* _____ soon.

fresh   2. A cold shower will _____ you.

marry   3. Did he _____ after his wife died?

fill   4. Let me _____ your glass.

produce   5. Can they _____ that painting?

fuel   6. Planes land here to _____.

build   7. Can you _____ that old engine?

live   8. I wish I could _____ those days.

union   9. Did he appear at the class _____?

heat   10. We can _____ that soup for lunch.

read   11. I want to _____ that book.

train   12. The factory will _____ its workers.

use   13. We can _____ these plastic forks.

place   14. _____ tires that appear worn.

new   15. I have to _____ my driver's license.

cycle   16. We can _____ beer and soda cans.

freeze   17. Cook the meat before you _____ it.

charge   18. The garage will _____ the battery.

write   19. Authors _____ stories many times.

elect   20. We hope to _____ him as president.

appear   21. After the storm, the sun will _____.

join   22. Please _____ us after your meeting.

assure   23. Good doctors _____ worried patients.

order   24. Phil had to _____ parts from the factory.

appoint   25. Did they _____ her for another term?

load   26. The hunter stopped to _____ his gun.

2 The prefix *re-* is also used before many words to give the meaning "back" or "backward."
Add *re-* to the words below, as shown in the first sentence.

turn   1. Phyllis will *return* _____ to college next fall.

call   2. Auto makers often _____ new cars.

act   3. How did Charlotte _____ to the news?

pay   4. Ralph says he will _____ the loan soon.

gain   5. A long rest helped her _____ her health.

fund   6. We asked the store to _____ our money.

wind   7. _____ the tape and then play it again.

coil   8. A gun will _____ when it is fired.

Practice 22-E: The Prefix *un-*

1 The prefix *un-* is often used before verbs
to mean "to do the opposite of."

Add *un-* to these verbs, as shown in the first sentence.

lock   1. Did you *unlock* the door?

cover   2. He wants to _____ the facts.

pack   3. When did Harry _____ his bags?

do   4. She tried to _____ the damage.

wrap   5. He is eager to _____ the gifts.

load   6. _____ the boxes from the truck.

dress   7. Charlene will _____ for bed.

---

2 The prefix *un-* is also used before adjectives.
Then *un-* means "not."

Add *un-* to these words, as in the first sentence.

fair   1. We thought the judge was *unfair*.

sure   2. George seems _____ of himself.

able   3. Charles was _____ to pass the test.

selfish   4. Mother is a very _____ person.

safe   5. That car is _____ to drive.

true   6. What he says is a lie. It's _____.

happy   7. Terry was _____ with his job.

usual   8. It's _____ for her to be late.

paid   9. The _____ bills are on the desk.

afraid   10. Ruth was _____ of the dangerous dog.

welcome   11. They made Warren feel _____.

known   12. For years, she was an _____ author.

Add *un-* to these words with endings like *-ed* and *-ly*.

married   13. That teacher is _____.

furnished   14. We rented an _____ apartment.

wanted   15. Some children feel _____.

employed   16. Many steel workers were _____.

expected   17. Some _____ guests dropped in on us.

finished   18. Joseph has some _____ business.

likely   19. It is _____ that he will quit his job.

friendly   20. The neighbors were _____ to us.

fortunate   21. We heard about his _____ accident.

pleasant   22. Michael's voice is loud and _____.

important   23. Don't worry about _____ things.

---

3 These words have the prefix *-un* and an ending. Read each word. Then underline the root word. The first word is done for you.

unwilling	unused	unhealthy	unanswered
uncooked	unlawful	unchanged	uninteresting
unlucky	unloved	unworthy	unfaithful

Practice 22-F: The Prefixes _dis-, im-, in-, non-_   **New words:** comfort, secret   **Review word:** report

The prefixes _dis-, im-, in-,_ and _non-_ are like the prefix _un-_. They mean "not" or "the opposite of."
Add the prefix to each word, and read the sentence.

1 dis-

agree   1. Did he _disagree_ with you?

approve   2. We _____ of Larry's friends.

appear   3. She watched the plane _____.

appoint   4. People sometimes _____ us.

cover   5. He could not _____ my secret.

courage   6. Don't let her words _____ you.

connect   7. Please _____ the phone.

continue   8. We must _____ these secret meetings.

obey   9. The children never _____ their father.

honest   10. The _____ man told many lies.

loyal   11. _____ friends spread your secrets.

comfort   12. Louis felt pain and _____.

2 im-

pure   1. Air in our cities is often _____.

possible   2. It was _____ to comfort the sick man.

patient   3. She is _____ with her little sister.

partial   4. Judges should be fair and _____.

3 in-

justice   1. Martin Luther King fought _____.

accurate   2. That report is _____.

correct   Many statements in it are _____.

human   3. Some jails are brutal and _____.

secure   4. I comfort my child if he feels _____.

direct   5. I had to take an _____ route to work.

efficient   6. Some office workers are _____.

sufficient   7. I had _____ funds to cover the check.

4 non-

fat   1. We drink _____ dry milk.

stop   2. Grace took a _____ flight to Chicago.

sense   3. That ghost story is _____.

fiction   4. Ginger likes to read _____ books.

smoking   5. Warren sat in the _____ section.

(Sometimes a hyphen is used with _non-,_ as in _a non-violent man_
or _non-prescription drugs._)

84

Practice 22-G: The Endings -able and -al

1 The ending -able is often added to verbs to make adjectives. The -able ending means "able to be" or "likely to be."

Add -able to these words, as shown in the first sentence. Don't forget to take off the final silent e before adding -able.

love
1. Her puppy is very ___lovable___ .

suit
2. Is that woman _____ for the job?

accept
3. That answer is not _____ .

value
4. Her jewels are quite _____ .

use
5. Are these toys still _____ ?

enjoy
6. It was an _____ party.

wash
7. Is this shirt _____ in hot water?

believe
8. Police think his story is _____ .

pleasure
9. We had a _____ vacation.

avoid
10. That accident was _____ .

employ
11. Are those workers _____ ?

train
12. Those animals are not _____ .

Do *not* drop the final e if the root word ends in -ce or -ge. The e is needed to show that c sounds like /s/ or that g sounds like /j/.

notice
13. That road sign is very ___noticeable___ .

peace
14. That country is _____ .

change
15. Her mood is _____ .

manage
16. Is the work _____ ?

2 Combine the prefix, the root word, and the ending -able, as shown.

(un) forgive (able) ➡ ___unforgivable___ sins

(un) break (able) ➡ _____ dishes

(un) manage (able) ➡ _____ children

(un) comfort (able) ➡ _____ chairs

(im) move (able) ➡ _____ mountains

(in) excuse (able) ➡ _____ mistake

(in) cure (able) ➡ _____ disease

3 The ending -al is often added to nouns to make adjectives. The -al ending means "related to" or "having to do with."

Add -al to these words. If there is a final silent e, drop the e before adding -al.

profession
1. She needs ___professional___ help.

person
2. He is a close _____ friend.

nation
3. New Year's Day is a _____ holiday.

nature
4. Coal and oil are _____ products.

emotion
5. Joseph has _____ problems.

tradition
6. _____ values are important to me.

brute
7. The killer was a _____ man.

occasion
8. We take an _____ vacation.

accident
9. Was her death _____ ?

85

Practice 23-A: *a* = /ə/ Alone in the First Syllable

1 The schwa sound

/ə/

a = /ə/ about

e = /ə/ taken

i = /ə/ pencil

o = /ə/ gallon

u = /ə/ circus

2

about	(a **bout**)	agree	(a **gree**)	among	(a **mong**)	awake	(a **wake**)
above	(a **bove**)	alone	(a **lone**)	adopt	(a **dopt**)	asleep	(a **sleep**)
across	(a **cross**)	along	(a **long**)	apart	(a **part**)	aware	(a **ware**)
adult	(a **dult**)	around	(a **round**)	alike	(a **like**)	amaze	(a **maze**)
afraid	(a **fraid**)	away	(a **way**)	alive	(a **live**)	award	(a **ward**)
again	(a **gain**)	amuse	(a **muse**)	alert	(a **lert**)	awhile	(a **while**)
against	(a **gainst**)	avoid	(a **void**)	aloud	(a **loud**)	apology	(a **pol** o gy)
ago	(a **go**)	ahead	(a **head**)	alarm	(a **larm**)	ability	(a **bil** i ty)

3 Read the sentences. **Review words:** afford, amount, arrest

1. Many adults are eager to adopt children.

2. The twins look alike. I can't tell them apart.

3. The little boy was afraid to go across the street alone.

4. To avoid being arrested, the thief ran away.

5. She was awake but not very alert when the alarm went off.

6. I agreed to go along with the plan. He voted against it.

7. The stories she tells about her children amuse us.

8. His sports ability earned him awards again and again.

9. I'm afraid I can't afford to buy a house around here.

10. Go ahead and pitch the tent among those trees.

11. We were amazed that he was alive after the accident.

12. The baby cried awhile before falling asleep.

13. She read her story aloud in the adult education class.

14. I'm aware of my mistakes. Please accept my apology.

15. We walked along the beach, looking around for shells.

16. A plane flew across the sky, high above us.

17. He avoids carrying around large amounts of money.

18. The cop was wide awake and alert, aware of every sound.

Practice 23-B: *a* = /ə/ **at the End of a Word**

1 a = /ə/

tuna
(**tu** na)

Cuba
(**Cu** ba)

America
(A **mer** i ca)

Carla
(**Car** la)

2

soda	(**so** da)	area	(**ar** e a)	Asia	(**A** sia)
sofa	(**so** fa)	camera	(**cam** er a)	Canada	(**Can** a da)
extra	(**ex** tra)	opera	(**op** er a)	Florida	(**Flor** i da)
drama	(**dra** ma)	idea	(i **de** a)	Africa	(**Af** ric a)
plaza	(**pla** za)	diploma	(di **plo** ma)	India	(**In** di a)
comma	(**com** ma)	vanilla	(va **nil** la)	Korea	(Ko **re** a)
china	(**chi** na)	banana	(ba **nan** a)	Alabama	(Al a **bam** a)
		pajamas	(pa **ja** mas)	California	(Cal i **for** nia)

Linda	(**Lin** da)
Donna	(**Don** na)
Laura	(**Lau** ra)
Martha	(**Mar** tha)
Sandra	(**San** dra)
Maria	(Ma **ri** a)
Barbara	(**Bar** ba ra)
Virginia	(Vir **gin** ia)

3 Read the sentences.   **Review words:** China, Rosa, Paula

1. Donna added some vanilla to the cookie dough.

2. Martha has many good ideas for the drama club.

3. Barbara was born in Alabama.

4. Virginia got her high school diploma at graduation.

5. Carla visited Africa, India, and China on her trip.

6. I'll have a tuna sandwich and a chocolate soda.

7. Asia is much bigger than North America.

8. Linda got a set of china as a wedding gift.

9. In California and Florida, the weather is usually warm.

10. Rosa fell asleep on the living room sofa.

11. Canada is the largest country in North America.

12. Sandra and Paula are going to the opera tonight.

13. Maria's family still lives in Cuba.

14. Laura made an extra loaf of banana bread.

15. Never put a comma at the end of a sentence.

16. This camera was made in South Korea.

17. The shopping plaza covers a big area.

18. These pajamas will keep you warm at night.

Practice 23-C: *a* = /ə/ **in Final Syllables**

1 **a = /ə/**

in final syllables

hospit<u>al</u>

fortun<u>ate</u>

hum<u>an</u>

import<u>ant</u>

insur<u>ance</u>

2

medal (**med** al)	criminal (**crim** i nal)	certain (**cer** tain)	organ (**or** gan)
metal (**met** al)	capital (**cap** i tal)	bargain (**bar** gain)	urban (**ur** ban)
national (**na** tion al)	principal (**prin** ci pal)	fountain (**foun** tain)	
personal (**per** son al)			balance (**bal** ance)
final (**fi** nal)	private (**pri** vate)	vacant (**va** cant)	appearance (ap **pear** ance)
local (**lo** cal)	climate (**cli** mate)	instant (**in** stant)	assistance (as **sis** tance)
signal (**sig** nal)	accurate (**ac** cu rate)	assistant (as **sis** tant)	performance (per **for** mance)
central (**cen** tral)	delicate (**del** i cate)	immigrant (**im** mi grant)	attendance (at **tend** ance)

3

Read the sentences.   **Review words:** breakfast, migrant, record, process

1. The assistant principal has a private office.

2. Attendance was good for the final performance.

3. The national swimming champ won a gold medal.

4. Are you certain that he has a criminal record?

5. At breakfast, Linda had a cup of instant coffee.

6. I bought a record of organ music. It was a bargain!

7. It's important for players to follow the coach's signals.

8. She needs assistance in filling out the insurance forms.

9. Our capital city is in the central part of the state.

10. Years ago, many immigrants moved into the urban areas.

11. The criminal was hiding out in the vacant building.

12. This personal information must be kept private.

13. The repairs improved the appearance of the local hospital.

14. My principal job is to be certain these facts are accurate.

15. There is a large fountain in Central Park.

16. It's fortunate that he did not lose his balance and fall.

17. The migrant workers moved on to states with warm climates.

18. Making rings from precious metals is a delicate process.

Practice 23-D: *a* = /ə/ **in the First or Middle Syllable**

1 **a = /ə/**

machine
(mạ **chine**)

paragraph
(**par** ạ graph)

alphabet
(**al** phạ bet)

2 **a = /ə/**
at the end of the first syllable

machine	(mạ **chine**)
canoe	(cạ **noe**)
canal	(cạ **nal**)
career	(cạ **reer**)
parade	(pạ **rade**)
patrol	(pạ **trol**)
garage	(gạ **rage**)
familiar	(fạ **mil** iar)

a = /ə/
in the middle of words

magazine	(mag ạ **zine**)	syllable	(**syl** lạ ble)
miracle	(**mir** ạ cle)	company	(**com** pạ ny)
probably	(**prob** ạ bly)	privacy	(**pri** vạ cy)
relative	(**rel** ạ tive)	vitamin	(**vi** tạ min)
theater	(**the** ạ ter)	sympathy	(**sym** pạ thy)
separate	(**sep** ạ rāte)	permanent	(**per** mạ nent)
diaper	(**di** ạ per)	marathon	(**mar** ạ thon)
diagram	(**di** ạ gram)	vegetable	(**veg** e tạ ble)

3 Read the sentences.   **New word:** return   **Review words:** salad, dictionary, highway

1. This diagram shows the parts of the machine.

2. Police patrol cars blocked off streets for the parade.

3. The marathon runner's picture was in the sports magazine.

4. Small boats and canoes went through the narrow canal.

5. Vegetable salads and fruit salads have lots of vitamins.

6. I saw many familiar faces at the class reunion.

7. Please return those tools to the garage.

8. That couple has separated. They will probably divorce.

9. His job with that company led to a permanent career.

10. Donna changed the baby's diapers.

11. In the dictionary, words are divided into syllables.

12. Roy will probably return to his acting job in the theater.

13. One of my relatives is a highway patrol officer.

14. We sent her a sympathy card when her father died.

15. She tried to separate her career from her personal life.

16. I returned to my office to have some privacy.

17. When his son was dying, Paul prayed for a miracle.

18. The magazine had photos of the New Year's Day parade.

89

Practice 23-E: *e* = /ə/

1   e = /ə/   2

1

cruel
(**cru** el)

different
(**dif** fer ent)

government
(**gov** ern ment)

avenue
(**av** e nue)

2

model (**mod** el)	diet (**di** et)	talent (**tal** ent)	basement (**base** ment)
novel (**nov** el)	quiet (**qui** et)	absent (**ab** sent)	moment (**mo** ment)
nickel (**nick** el)	blanket (**blank** et)	innocent (**in** no cent)	compliment (**com** pli ment)
travel (**trav** el)	toilet (**toi** let)	detergent (de **ter** gent)	instrument (**in** stru ment)
shovel (**shov** el)	dozen (**doz** en)	resident (**res** i dent)	appointment (ap **point** ment)
label (**la** bel)	beaten (**beat** en)	science (**sci** ence)	calendar (**cal** en dar)
cancel (**can** cel)	siren (**si** ren)	influence (**in** flu ence)	bulletin (**bul** le tin)
channel (**chan** nel)	citizen (**cit** i zen)	experience (ex **per** i ence)	envelope (**en** ve lope)

3   Read the sentences.   **Review words:** residence, difference, recent, cleaner, several

1. Wait a moment. I'll check the appointments on my calendar.

2. Our science club has a poster on the bulletin board.

3. Martha put labels on dozens of envelopes.

4. Put the toilet bowl cleaner and detergents on this shelf.

5. Did they cancel the TV show at noon on channel 5?

6. He was beaten in the game by a more experienced player.

7. The model tried many different diets to lose weight.

8. I sat in a quiet place to read my science fiction novel.

9. What's the difference in price between these two blankets?

10. He played several instruments in the recent talent show.

11. Her classroom is quiet today because many kids are absent.

12. I moved from my basement apartment to a larger residence.

13. Many immigrants who traveled to the U.S. became citizens.

14. We heard sirens as police cars raced down the avenue.

15. He got several compliments on the model car he built.

16. Take the shovel and garden tools down to the basement.

17. City residents can influence their government by voting.

18. I saw my son steal a nickel, but he says he is innocent.

Practice 23-F: *i* = /ə/

1 i = /ə/

visit
(**vis** it)

notice
(**no** tice)

animal
(**an** i mal)

possible
(**pos** si ble)

2

divide	(di **vide**)	profit	(**prof** it)	policy	(**pol** i cy)	uniform	(**u** ni form)
direct	(di **rect**)	promise	(**prom** ise)	politics	(**pol** i tics)	confident	(**con** fi dent)
divorce	(di **vorce**)	evil	(**e** vil)	imitate	(**im** i tate)	multiply	(**mul** ti ply)
		gossip	(**gos** sip)	hesitate	(**hes** i tate)	attitude	(**at** ti tude)
exit	(**ex** it)			qualify	(**qual** i fy)	quantity	(**quan** ti ty)
habit	(**hab** it)	holiday	(**hol** i day)	evidence	(**ev** i dence)	intelligent	(in **tel** li gent)
limit	(**lim** it)	editor	(**ed** i tor)	positive	(**pos** i tive)	institution	(in sti **tu** tion)
spirit	(**spir** it)	quality	(**qual** i ty)	charity	(**char** i ty)	anniversary	(an ni **ver** sa ry)

---

3 Read the sentences.   **Review words:** easily, terrible

1. He promised to give part of his profits to charity.

2. Did you notice the speed limit sign on the exit ramp?

3. School spirit is high among students at this institution.

4. She has a terrible habit of spreading evil gossip.

5. Police were directing traffic on the divided highway.

6. Our newspaper editor wants quality as well as quantity.

7. This insurance policy cannot be understood easily.

8. She is an intelligent woman with a positive attitude.

   I'm confident that she can succeed in politics.

9. I don't think I qualify for the job. I hesitate to apply.

10. We celebrated our wedding anniversary over the holiday.

11. The teacher taught the children to multiply and divide.

12. I'm positive he's innocent. I have evidence to prove it.

13. In institutions like hospitals, employees wear uniforms.

14. Smoking is a terrible habit. I promise I'll try to quit.

15. It is possible to get a quick divorce in some states.

16. Children need positive models to imitate.

17. Company policy allows employees to have holidays off.

Practice 23-G: *o* = /ə/

1 o = /ə/

2

carrot
(**car** rot)

gallon
(**gal** lon)

confuse
(**con** fuse)

occur
(**oc** cur)

riot	(**ri** ot)	prison	(**pris** on)	compare	(com **pare**)	observe	(ob **serve**)
ballot	(**bal** lot)	wagon	(**wag** on)	complain	(com **plain**)	obtain	(ob **tain**)
pilot	(**pi** lot)	bacon	(**ba** con)	complete	(com **plete**)	tomato	(to **ma** to)
bottom	(**bot** tom)	carton	(**car** ton)	community	(com **mu** ni ty)	ignorant	(**ig** no rant)
custom	(**cus** tom)	apron	(**a** pron)	concern	(con **cern**)	violent	(**vi** o lent)
freedom	(**free** dom)	cotton	(**cot** ton)	control	(con **trol**)	violin	(vi o **lin**)
seldom	(**sel** dom)	common	(**com** mon)	consent	(con **sent**)	violate	(**vi** o late)
method	(**meth** od)	reason	(**rea** son)	conserve	(con **serve**)	period	(**per** i od)

3 Read the sentences.   **Review word:** million

1. She wrote in a name on the bottom of the ballot.

2. He had to obtain his parent's consent to drive.

3. Millions of people are concerned about conserving energy.

4. He has taken violin lessons for a long period.

5. A violent riot broke out in the prison.

6. Decorating trees is a common custom at Christmas.

7. The pilot was in complete control of the plane.

8. Carla got some bacon grease on her cotton apron.

9. We loaded large cartons of books into the station wagon.

10. Observe the speed limit, or you will violate the law.

11. I bought a gallon of ice cream and a carton of milk.

12. They are ignorant of many community services.

13. He seldom complains. When he does, he has a good reason.

14. Add a tomato and some carrots to that salad.

15. I observed that he seldom compares prices when he shops.

16. People in our community are concerned about crime control.

17. Complete the test and hand it in at the end of the period.

18. They never used violent methods in the fight for freedom.

Practice 23-H: *u* = /ə/

1   u = /ə/

support
(sup **port**)

minute
(**min** ute)

campus
(**cam** pus)

museum
(mu **se** um)

2

support	(sup **port**)	syrup	(**syr** up)	museum	(mu **se** um)
supply	(sup **ply**)	minute	(**min** ute)	medium	(**me** di um)
suppose	(sup **pose**)			stadium	(**sta** di um)
suspect	(sus **pect**)	campus	(**cam** pus)	maximum	(**max** i mum)
suspend	(sus **pend**)	circus	(**cir** cus)	minimum	(**min** i mum)
suspense	(sus **pense**)	virus	(**vi** rus)		
suggest	(sug **gest**)	insult	(**in** sult)	industry	(**in** dus try)
subtract	(sub **tract**)	difficult	(**dif** fi cult)	volunteer	(vol un **teer**)

3

Read the sentences.   **Review word:** subject

1. She poured syrup over the waffles.

2. He left campus after he was suspended from school.

3. Did you volunteer to take the kids to the circus?

4. The stadium holds a maximum of fifty thousand people.

5. Doctors suspect that the disease is caused by a virus.

6. This steak is medium rare, but it is difficult to cut.

7. He can't support himself on a job paying minimum wage.

8. That industry will supply jobs for many workers.

9. I can't stand this suspense for another minute.

10. A volunteer tutor taught the child to add and subtract.

11. He suggested that I was lazy! What an insult!

12. Art is her best subject, and she loves to visit museums.

13. That game is difficult. Who do you suppose will win?

14. She loves suspense novels. Can you suggest a good one?

15. Fifty-five miles an hour is the maximum speed limit.

16. The minute we begin to argue, I try to change the subject.

17. I suspect that the steel industry will lay off more workers.

18. Her husband is supposed to send money for child support.

Practice 24-A: Vowel Endings on Words of Two or More Syllables

1 Some word endings begin with a vowel (-*ing*, -*ed*, -*er*, -*est*, -*en*, -*able*, -*al*).
You know how to add them to one-syllable words. If the word ends in CVC, double the last consonant.

What if you want to add these endings to words of two or more syllables that end with CVC?
Double the last consonant if the stress is on the *last* syllable of the root word.

cvc
slip + **p** + [vowel ending] ➞ **slipping**
slipped
slipper

admit (ad **mit**)   The stress is on the last syllable, so double: admitting, admitted

visit (**vis** it)   The stress is *not* on the last syllable. Don't double: visiting, visited

---

2 Add -*ed* to each word.

commit (com **mit**) _____

prefer (pre **fer**) _____

happen (**hap** pen) _____

rebel (re **bel**) _____

wander (**wan** der) _____

prohibit (pro **hib** it) _____

3 Add -*ing* to each word.

control (con **trol**) _____

offer (**of** fer) _____

refer (re **fer**) _____

remember (re **mem** ber) _____

color (**col** or) _____

begin (be **gin**) _____

4 Add the ending shown.

forbid (for **bid**) + en _____

open (**o** pen) + er _____

labor (**la** bor) + er _____

regret (re **gret**) + able _____

honor (**hon** or) + able _____

season (**sea** son) + al _____

---

5 Mark the stressed syllable in the root word. Then add -*ed*.

permit (per mít)   *permitted*

limit (lim it) _____

occur (oc cur) _____

wonder (won der) _____

deposit (de pos it) _____

6 Mark the stressed syllable in the root word. Then add -*ing*.

listen (lis ten) _____

upset (up set) _____

patrol (pa trol) _____

poison (poi son) _____

forget (for get) _____

7 Mark the stressed syllable in the root word. Then add the ending shown.

begin (be gin) + er _____

reason (rea son) + able _____

control (con trol) + able _____

profit (prof it) + able _____

forgot (for got) + en _____

Practice 24-B: Final Syllable *le*

1 CC-le (double consonant)

apple	bottle	waffle
(**ap** ple)	(**bot** tle)	(**waf** fle)

Read the word first. Then read the sentence.

1. middle   (**mid** dle)   I'm in the <u>middle</u> of this book.

2. bubble   (**bub** ble)   Phyllis took a <u>bubble</u> bath.

3. settle   (**set** tle)   He will never <u>settle</u> down.

4. struggle   (**strug** gle)   I had to <u>struggle</u> hard to win.

5. ruffle   (**ruf** fle)   That blouse has a lace <u>ruffle</u>.

6. puzzle   (**puz** zle)   This <u>puzzle</u> has many pieces.

3 CC-le (-*ckle*, -*ngle*, -*nkle*)

buckle	single	ankle
(**buck** le)	(**sin** gle)	(**an** kle)
	(**sin[g]** gle)	(**an[g]** kle)

Read the word. Fill in the blank. Then read the sentence.

1. tackle   (**tack** le)   Did Paul _____ the football player?

2. pickle   (**pick** le)   We opened a jar of sweet _____s.

3. angle   (**an** gle)   Soon, the road will _____ to the left.

4. jungle   (**jun** gle)   Many wild animals live in the _____.

5. wrinkle   (**wrin** kle)   Iron the _____s out of that blouse.

6. sprinkle   (**sprin** kle)   _____ water on the flowers.

2 CC-le (different consonants)

simple	sparkle	whistle
(**sim** ple)	(**spar** kle)	(**whis** *t*le)

Read the word first. Then read the sentence.

1. gamble   (**gam** ble)   Phil <u>gambles</u> his money away.

2. startle   (**star** tle)   Did that noise <u>startle</u> you?

3. purple   (**pur** ple)   Fill the basket with <u>purple</u> grapes.

4. handle   (**han** dle)   I grabbed the pail by the <u>handle</u>.

5. turtle   (**tur** tle)   The <u>turtle</u> has a hard shell.

6. circle   (**cir** cle)   We sat in a <u>circle</u> around her.

7. gentle   (**gen** tle)   He spoke in a <u>gentle</u> voice.

8. wrestle   (**wres** tle)   The boys like to <u>wrestle</u> together.

4 VC-le

able	bugle	needle	poodle
(**ā** ble)	(**bū** gle)	(**nēē** dle)	(**poo** dle)

Fill in each blank with one of these -*le* words.

cradle	(**cra** dle)
rifle	(**ri** fle)
maple	(**ma** ple)
stable	(**sta** ble)
title	(**ti** tle)
eagle	(**ea** gle)
beetle	(**bee** tle)
noodle	(**noo** dle)

1. What is the *title* of that book?

2. A _____ crawled under the rug.

3. The hunter aimed his _____.

4. We get sap from _____ trees.

5. Rock the baby in the _____.

6. Have some chicken _____ soup.

7. The _____ flew up to its nest.

8. She put the horses in the _____.

Practice 24-C: Compound Words

1 Find the two smaller words in each compound word. Write them in the blanks, as shown. Read the words.

homework _home_ _work_

landlord _____ _____

forever _____ _____

anyway _____ _____

understand _____ _____

cookbook _____ _____

downtown _____ _____

granddaughter _____ _____

2 Make as many compound words as you can by putting together a word on the left with a word on the right. Two have been done for you. (Do not list *no one* as a compound word because it is two words.)

anybody _____ _____

anyone _____ _____

any	body
every	one
some	thing
no	where

_____ _____ _____

_____ _____ _____

2 Make compound words by putting each word on the left with a word on the right. Write the compound word in the blank. The first one is done for you.

tooth _toothache_ point

some _____ print

view _____ how

blue _____ ache

law _____ neck

bull _____ suit

rough _____ board

chalk _____ frog

cross _____ knob

break _____ wash

mouth _____ walk

door _____ through

3 Use these compound words to fill in the blanks:

| bathroom | nightgown | overdrawn | scrapbook | spellbound | washcloth | waterproof | wristwatch |

1. My checking account is _____ again!

2. Joyce bought a lovely pink _____.

3. We sat _____ through the movie.

4. A _____ and some towels are in the _____.

5. Gene put the photographs in the _____.

6. Paul's _____ keeps good time. Is it _____?

96